Addiction:
Saved by the Grace of God

Addiction: Saved by the Grace of God

The Anthony Marakovitz Story

ANTHONY MARAKOVITZ

Edited by Krissie Schuster Cilano

Foreword by Sharon Ciano

RESOURCE *Publications* · Eugene, Oregon

ADDICTION: SAVED BY THE GRACE OF GOD
The Anthony Marakovitz Story

Resource Publications
An Imprint of Wipf and Stock Publishers
199 W. 8th Ave., Suite 3
Eugene, OR 97401

www.wipfandstock.com

PAPERBACK ISBN: 979-8-3852-0963-7
HARDCOVER ISBN: 979-8-3852-0964-4
EBOOK ISBN: 979-8-3852-0965-1

02/28/24

To my mother and father and my beloved grandfather, "Maka"
Thank you.

"But those who wait on the LORD will find new strength. They will fly high on wings like eagles. They will run and not grow weary. They will walk and not faint."

ISAIAH 40:31 NIV

Contents

CONTENTS

Foreword

TONY CAME INTO MY family's life over eleven years ago. At first, we all wondered what Gerry, my girlfriend of forty years, was thinking when she introduced her finance, a big, bald, tattooed guy from New Jersey who spoke Jerseyeeze—a recovering alcoholic and drug addict, with no home, no car, and no money. What an odd choice for my friend! As time went by, Tony revealed the kind, loving, and trusting man that he is. He embraces life and all that it offers, taking one day at a time. He became an instant family man, father, grandfather, and good friend to me and my family and to all who have met him, excited to begin a new chapter in his life. His large wingspan tells it all. He's filled with love. He cares about people and hopes to be a shining example to all who meet him.

Tony's book will make you laugh and cry. He will take you on an adventure of telling real stories that will amaze you. I have met some of the people in this book who have touched Tony's life from childhood to adulthood.

Enjoy this remarkable story and watch the transformation take place in his life on an emotional and spiritual level. If you don't believe in God and the miracles He performs, you will by the time you finish this book.

SHARON CIANO

Acknowledgments

I AM GRATEFUL TO God for His hand in putting this book together. He has granted me many friendships of gifted people along the way. Certainly, the love and encouragement I continually experience in my life with Christ are reflected in these pages. Much encouragement came from people who afforded me unconditional love—my original family, my current family, the family of God who are members and leaders from various church denominations and recovery programs, and faithful followers of Christ who continue to seek, as well as to teach others to seek, the lost.

Many thanks to the professionals at Wipf and Stock Publishers who accepted our proposal to publish this book, believing that my story would benefit others. Your patience and know-how were an enormous blessing to us!

Many thanks to you who share God's goodness, mercy, and love by serving others and by believing that there is *always* hope in Him.

Blessings,

ANTHONY "TONY" MARAKOVITZ

Abbreviations

Bible translations for Scripture references:

(AMP) the AMPLIFIED® BIBLE
(KJV) King James Version
(MSG) THE MESSAGE
(NIV) New International Version
(NLT) New Living Translation

Other abbreviations:

AA Alcoholics Anonymous
CDL Commercial Driver's License
CEO Chief Executive Officer
CPA Certified Public Accountant
CPR Cardiopulmonary Resuscitation
CR Celebrate Recovery
DEA Drug Enforcement Administration
DMV Department of Motor Vehicles
DUI Driving under the influence (of alcohol or drugs)
HIV Human Immunodeficiency Virus
IRS Internal Revenue Service
K2 synthetic marijuana
LLC limited liability company
Oxys oxycodone
UFO unidentified flying object

Introduction

"Hi. My name is Anthony, and I am a true believer in the Lord Jesus Christ. I struggle with drugs, alcohol, anger, pride, ego, gambling, sexual integrity, codependency, and the list goes on. I have a disease called the addiction of more." These were my own words when I was asked to "make a searching and fearless moral inventory of myself" as a Fourth Step toward my recovery—after forty years of addictions.

I would like to share my story of where I was and where I am now, to give hope to those who suffer from addictions of any kind. My prayer is to touch as many lives as I can with my message of hope before I leave this earth.

And, to clear the air—this is my side of the street. I chose my actions. Nobody forced my actions on me, and I don't condemn anyone in my story. This story has nothing to do with them; it's my story, the way I was taught in my Twelve Steps to Recovery. I want everyone to know that God was with me all the way, and He let me see clearly that my past was a training for my future!

Chapter 1

That's Amore

MY MOTHER AND FATHER met on St. Anthony's Feast Day, June 13, 1955, in Lyndhurst, New Jersey. It was a feast that my Uncle Joe used to have in his backyard for Our Lady of Carmel Church. Uncle Joe was married to my mother's sister, MaryAnn. He was my Uncle Joe "Pags," a bookie in New York—an "earner," they would say.

Who knows for sure who saw the other one first? My guess is that my dad was hanging out there, just being his "cool cat" self in his leather jacket, rolled-up jeans, a cigarette in his mouth, and slicked-back hair. This was only a few years after Marlon Brando (dressed just like my dad) starred in *The Wild One* (1953), and about the same time James Dean thrilled girls with the same look in *Rebel Without a Cause* (1955). At 6'2" my dad was a lankier version of those guys. My dad's friends called him "Slim," but his real name was Henry Marakovitz after his Austrian-American father who owned H. Marakovitz and Sons Painting and Decorating Company. That day my dad was freefalling fast in love with Lucy Margotta, a dark-haired, American-Sicilian girl. She probably never even noticed him with his 50's greaser look. He was eighteen; she was seventeen, and I was only a sparkle in his incandescent eyes.

Slim and Lucy started dating, dancing to jukebox music, drinking sodas in the Mamba Room near the high school, and "digging" the music with their friends in East Rutherford, New

Jersey. They hung out at carnivals and festivals sponsored by the Catholic churches, too, where there were always massive amounts of authentic Italian food, bright lights, happy people, and lots of activity. From blocks away, robust whiffs of sizzling sausages with peppers and onions, meatballs, pasta, fried dough, and pizza dominated the air with plenty of loud, live music. The thought makes my mouth water even now.

Eventually, Lucy and Slim were engaged, and, as the story goes, my grandmother (my father's mother) passed away too soon from alcoholism, leaving my young grandfather alone to run the business and take care of their boys—my dad and his brother Ronald "Rocky." My mother's idea was to get married earlier than planned so that she could take care of my widowed grandfather and my uncle Rocky who was sixteen at the time. Besides that, she wanted to get out of the chaos she was living in at home under the thumb of her alcoholic stepfather.

My mother's mother and father were another story. My mother's mother was born on a boat coming from Sicily to the New York Harbor. She married and had five children with her first husband whose name was Canio Margotta. One time, at a barbecue at McDonald's Lake in Wayne, New Jersey, some of the people got terribly sick. Turns out, someone had brought to the barbecue some peppers that had been preserved in jars at home, and Canio, my mother's father, who was probably thirty-five years old when this happened, was one of more than ten people who died from botulism! My mother's Aunt Lily, my grandmother's sister, was the only one who ate those peppers and survived. She had a scar on her neck showing where a doctor performed a tracheotomy that saved her life. Not wallowing in grief or blaming God, my mother's mother moved on, and three of her eight children shared my mom's stepfather's different last name. No one blamed my grandmother for that. She needed help with the five children that she already had. At an early age, my mom learned how precious and fragile life could be, and how faith in God could help people move forward. My mother was accurately described by many as small in stature with a gigantic heart full of love, loyalty, and faith.

In November of 1955, Dad was wearing a cummerbund and a tux with one white rose in his satin lapel. My mother was his radiant better half wearing a graceful, white lace gown and pearl drop earrings. In her hands was a cascade of orchids and white roses, and in her high heels and bouffant hair under a floral veil, she stood taller than usual—only a pinch below my father's shoulder, a height that must've caused a few doubletakes and comments, "Is that really our Lucy?" Months of preparation went into their formal wedding at St. Joseph's Church; my mother's sisters and friends were all in the wedding party. Clearly happy, the newlyweds vowed to love each other forever, come what may. They were both sure that they had found The Right One!

Mom and Dad's wedding day, 1955

3

After the wedding, my Uncle Rocky, my grandfather Henry (who later became "Maka" when I came into the world), and my mom and dad all moved into a two-story, two-bedroom, one-bath house on Grove Street in East Rutherford, New Jersey. There was a backyard but no garage, and the Barkers, a family of six (three girls and one boy) lived above us. On March 3, 1957, at 4:43 in the afternoon, God brought me into this world at Beth Israel Hospital in Passaic, New Jersey, and my family carried me to our first home on Grove Street. My mother was loving and protective of me. She even polished my baby shoes and replaced the laces while I slept. I was the cleanest baby in town.

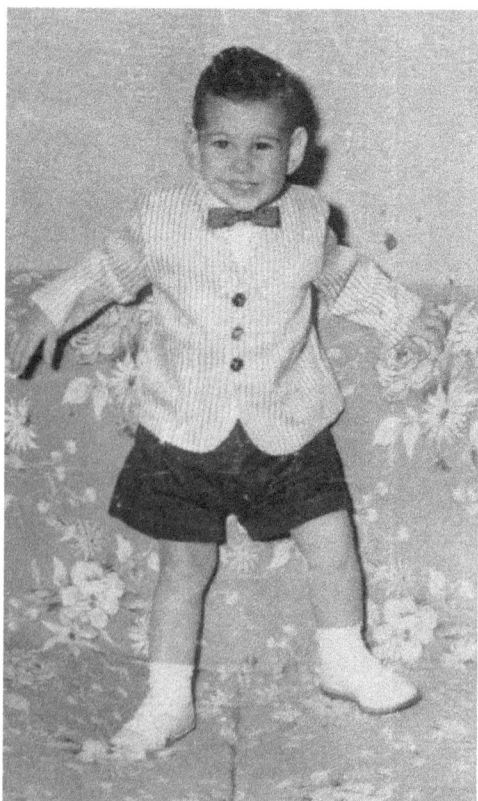

The cleanest baby in town!

I have flashbacks of Christmas there: me in my striped pajamas at midnight, heading toward dunes of unwrapped Christmas presents under the tree and a house full of people who were happy to be there. Traditionally, everyone loudly welcomed each other with plenty of hugs and kisses. And, always there was one unavoidable lobster greeting coming from my grandma who would grab my face by the cheeks between her thumbs and forefingers before planting a schmacker of a kiss on my forehead—"Mmmwah!" and touting, "Anthony! What a handsome boy!"

me with Grandma

There were casseroles, dishes, bowls, bottles, trays, and tables full of specially-made Italian food, even the traditional Italian seven fishes, throughout the smoky night until morning while my

5

father angled around everyone trying to take it all into his 8mm movie camera. All the films were titled and dated: *Anthony crawling under the Christmas tree, Anthony playing under the Christmas tree, Anthony playing in the snow, Anthony on the trampolines in Wildwood, New Jersey.* Hours and hours of my early years were on film for everyone to watch—all my father's friends, my mother's friends, too, my Aunt Tootsie (my father's sister) and Uncle Don Tatham (married to my Aunt Tootsie), and Mr. and Mrs. Tatham (Uncle Don's mother and father), Red and Ro-Ro Greenleaf, Carl Conrad, Joey "Cass" Cassiere, and my mother's sisters, Aunt Paula, Aunt Frannie, and Aunt MaryAnn, married to my uncle Joe "Pags."

I was named after Saint Anthony because my mother and father met at Saint Anthony's Feast. I didn't know it at the time, but Saint Anthony was the patron saint of anything lost—purses, car keys, souls, people—anything and anyone. My middle name Joseph came from the best man at the wedding, Joey Cassiere ("Joey Cass"), a gifted drummer who lived next door to us on Grove Street and played the drums for Frankie Valli and the Four Seasons in the Sixties. He didn't stay with the Four Seasons when they went on the road, though. Instead, he left the band because he got homesick. He came back home and played the drums for commercials in NYC and had steady paychecks coming to his mailbox. Joey Cass, my godfather, was my idol. He taught me how to play drums.

We moved from Grove Street in East Rutherford to a town next door, Carlstadt, New Jersey, when I was three years old. Our new place was a single-family house with three bedrooms, one bath, a large yard, and a garage for my grandfather's car, my dad's car and truck, and my Uncle Rocky's car. Our family was still H. Marakovitz and Sons Painting and Decorating Company. I shared a room in our house on Hackensack Street with my grandfather until I was twenty-four years old. My mother, father, Uncle Rocky, and my grandfather always welcomed my friends into our home. There was plenty of room and plenty of happiness, fun, love, and joy in our home. A wonderful life for all of us!

Everyone went somewhere every morning. My grandfather, dad, and Uncle Rocky went to work at our painting and decorating company; my mother did the shopping and housework, and I went to my first school days at Washington Elementary School in 1963.

One day, not long after school began that year, everyone in our school was sent home. I didn't mind going home early, in fact, I was probably hoping my Aunt Paula would be there to watch *Felix the Cat* on TV with me. My Aunt Paula was my mother's little sister, only six years older than I was, so she was like a big sister to me who stayed at our house a lot. We used to eat potato chips and drink milk together on our sofa while watching TV for hours. When I got home that day, the TV was already on, but Aunt Paula wasn't there, and *Felix the Cat* wasn't on our TV either.

The only thing on TV that day, and for days to come, was about the President of the United States. Even the people who were trying to do the news couldn't hold back their tears because they had to tell everyone that the President of the United States had died. The same news played over and over. My father kept telling me to look at the President's little boy who was standing with his mother and sister on the street when the funeral procession passed by them with soldiers and horses walking in front of and behind loud drums and slow, sad music. The little boy must have loved his father. When we saw the newsclip of him saluting his dad, we saluted too. Right there in our living room we stood up with that little boy, John John, and saluted the passing of the first Catholic President in our country.

Everyone under our roof was a Catholic. I started wearing a suit to church the minute I was out of my mother's arms. My mother and father taught me that God was loving and that we should do things the right way, the loving way. We never blamed God if things didn't go right. We didn't question Him, either. We lived loving each other. I was brought up believing in God the Father and Jesus the Son. My mother was heavy into Catholicism and came from a family of four boys and four girls. We ate fish on Fridays and went to church on Sundays, which, became known as "Macaroni Sundays," because my mother served macaroni with meatballs, red sauce, and chunks of crusty, warm Italian bread every Sunday after church.

Apparently, it didn't occur to me that I was going to school to learn to read and write or to learn anything else. All my friends were there, so we met on the playground and had a good time in class all day long. None of us ever suspected that the teacher was grading us! I found out about it when they kept me back in third grade. My mom went to school to talk to my teacher who said I hadn't learned anything since day one. So, my mother took me out of that school and enrolled me in the third grade at Lindburgh Elementary School on the other side of town where I had to find all new friends. That upset me until I found out that my new teacher, Mrs. Kutcher, was a dream come true! She made learning fun! My friends and I wrote a play with the Charlie Brown puppets that we made in class. In our play, aliens landed in a UFO and took all of us away. The class loved it. Later, in a school play about Snow White, I was given the role of "Dopey," one of the seven dwarfs. The Bergen County newspaper said I was so funny that I stole the show.

Summertime meant no school for a few months. In the late 50's and 60's, music was the Motown sound. My mother played Motown on the car radio on our fifteen-minute drive to my Aunt MaryAnn and Aunt Frannie's beauty parlor, the White Oak Beauty Salon, in Nutley, NJ, where Frankie Valli was born. I learned the rhythms and words to all the songs by the Supremes and the Temptations, and I remember sitting in the front seat of the car—no seatbelt, just a hula hoop on the dashboard that I used as a steering wheel to pretend I was driving while belting out Motown songs with my mother. My aunts' salon was always packed with women whose heads were under barrel-shaped hairdryers. Others were having their hair styled or their makeup and nails done. I played outside with some friends while my mom washed rollers, combs, and brushes for her sisters.

For ten days at the end of every summer, my mother and her cousin Lucy (married to Joey Cass) and I went to the beach in Wildwood, New Jersey, where we stayed at Shaw's Apartments near the Boardwalk. My dad came only on the weekends because he had to work. The Shaws were close friends of our family, so they babysat me while my family went to the clubs to hear Joey Cass play the drums with his band. Those were the days when oceanside boardwalks and parks were big draws because all the fun was in one place—wide, sandy beaches on the ocean, thrilling rides, great food everywhere, bicycles, trams, hundreds of vendors on the piers, laughing friends, and great entertainment in beach clubs, nightclubs, and supper clubs that billed celebrities, like Tony Bennett, Fats Domino, Little Richard, Frank Sinatra, Dean Martin, and Dick Clark. People waited all year long for their summer vacations in Wildwood, NJ, where everywhere was fun all the time, and no one ever got homesick!

As I grew up, my mother let me know about doing things that God might punish me for, like lying, stealing, and saying "bad" words. My dad repeated his warnings about how his mother died from alcoholism. I found out about my dad's work belt that kept me from doing things I shouldn't, like letting the air out of my dad's tires (as a joke), then blaming some guy who was walking down the street, or playing with matches or fireworks. My mother used to chase me through the house, waving her wooden spoon and warning me, "Just wait 'til your *father* gets home, Anthony!" That meant "the work belt." One time I ran and hid inside my toybox when I heard my dad coming with his work belt. When he saw all my toys on the floor, he knew where I was. He lifted the lid of the toybox, and there I was, looking at him with such fear on my face that apparently he couldn't handle it. He stooped down and picked me up. Then, in a surprising move, he held me, dropped his work belt, and hugged me so passionately that it seemed like he was sorrier than I was for whatever it was that I had done. Years later my dad told me that he wished he hadn't broken my bicycle when he caught me riding it in the street after I'd been told a million times *not* to ride my bicycle in the street. It must've haunted him forever that he made me cry after he did that.

A young Franciscan Catholic priest from nearby Saint Joseph's Church came to our house a lot to spend time with my mother and father and to bless us and our home. They'd talk over coffee. The priest was maybe thirty years old when I was six, the perfect age for me to start classes called CCD (Confraternity of Christian Doctrine)—simply "catechism," religious education for Catholic kids who attended secular schools. We learned about God and memorized prayers like The Our Father and The Hail Mary, a Catholic prayer asking the Virgin Mary, the mother of Jesus, to intercede for all sinners and to communicate with God on their (our) behalf. I knew the words but had no idea what they meant or where these people we were praying to were. The routine was Catechism, First Holy Communion at age six or seven, followed by Confirmation at age thirteen or fourteen. I loved that priest and wanted to be like him. They called him Father Mike who later became known as Father Mychal Judge.

No one on earth could have known then that Father Mychal would become the Chaplain of the New York City Fire Department one day, and that the final moments of his sixty-eight years of life on earth would be on the morning of September 11, 2001. There's a famous photo of Father Mychal being carried through thick bomb dust by five sweating, grimy, heartbroken New York City firemen who found his body in the rubble. He became known as the first certified fatality of the September 11th attacks, "Fatality 0001." Father Mychal's fire helmet was presented to Pope John Paul II, France awarded him the Legion of Honor, and he was nominated for the Congressional Gold Medal as well as for the Presidential Medal of Freedom. Not only that, but the City of New York renamed a portion of West 31st Street "Father Mychal F. Judge Street" where he lived in the friary. New York City honored him further by christening a commuter ferry "The Father Mychal Judge" in 2002, the same year that the US Congress passed into law, The Mychal Judge Police and Fire Chaplains Public Safety Officers Benefit Act, which extended federal benefits to surviving families, retroactive to September 11, 2001. In that same year, the Orthodox Catholic Church of America canonized him, and he became known as Saint Mychal the Martyr.

Imagine that. In 1967, when I was ten years old, Father Mychal, my idol, was at our kitchen table in my house drinking coffee with my mom and dad, blessing our home and family before he became a saint!

> *"LORD, take me where You want me to go, let me meet who You want me to meet,*
> *Tell me what You want me to say, and keep me out of Your way. Amen."*
> Prayer of Saint Mychal Judge[1]

1 "Mychal Judge" Wikimedia .2010.

Chapter 2

That Awkward Age

ALL THE WAY THROUGH elementary school until the end of seventh grade, I was in Lindburgh Elementary School. After that, everyone in the surrounding county went to a brand-new school for eighth grade only. The new Washington Middle School was built on the site of what was previously Washington Elementary School. Graduating from this school was a big deal before going to Henry P. Becton High School for grades nine through twelve. Finally, I was back with all my old friends! It was a long-awaited reunion after which we became inseparable: Chuck Routar, Jimmy Renke, Joe Trenery, Tommy Kamphausen, Paul Bradley, Mike Beggs, Mike Paparella, and Joey Pandorf. We hung out in basketball courts and with the girls too. I'd moved past catechism classes, confirmation hurdles, confessions of any kind, and even Father Mychal. I didn't have to go to church if I didn't want to, so I didn't go. Manhood began—something I'd waited for all my life!

My buddies and I formed a group called The Junior Mafia. My friend's father, Mr. Paparella, owned a big, four-family house on Hackensack Street across from where I lived. From behind this house on the side of a hill, the New York City skyline was visible. That's where we brainstormed about building a fort for our gang.

On foggy, rainy nights we'd go out looking for houses that were being built so we could steal wood and other supplies that were lying around those sites. We'd be running with 2x4s, ply-wood, and insulation through the wet streets of Carlstadt to build our fort. One room had 8' ceilings and about 25' x 25' of paneling on the walls with full power, lights, and sockets. Mike Beggs' father was an electrician, so Mike got everything from his dad, put power in, and ran it to the pole. The other room was a bunk room with nine bunk beds built into three walls. We spent weekends there just hanging out.

We were always in trouble and repeatedly wound up in school suspension. The teachers gave us homework and kept us in a room that was the size of a closet for the rest of the day. Suspension lasted only a couple of days. Long story short: we all graduated eighth grade by the skin of our teeth.

Our eighth-grade graduation was big. My mother and father reserved a table for us that night at Ott's Spot, where they normally went on Friday nights to see my godfather Joey Cass and his band. That night my mother, father, and their friends Vinny and Betty were our chaperones. Most of my parents' other friends were cops who were there too. The band played a dance for us graduates. I wore my first tux that night, and my date was a pretty girl named Tina.

At fifteen years old we started drinking alcohol at our parties. My friend Tommy's brother took our money and picked up liquor for us. When we got some pot and tried it for the first time, we loved it! I fit in with the crowd. We loved drinking whatever was available, smoking pot, and partying with the "women." Things were really happening; I was becoming a Big Shot.

One night we got raided at our fort by the Carlstadt Police Department. Luckily, no one had any pot, just some Boone's Farm wine, Colt 45 Malt Liquor, and Strawberry Hill, (also wine), so we were cited only for drinking under age. Our parents had to come to the police station to get us. My parents didn't kill me. They just told me not to do it again. The worst part of it all was we had to rip down the fort.

So, what did I do? I built a room in the basement like the back of a custom van with a heart-shaped bed, couches, cool lighting, and a stereo, and we were ready for the parties to start up again. My parents respected my privacy by not going down there. They figured we couldn't get into trouble in the basement. They weren't aware that we were sneaking liquor through the basement window and smoking pot outside. Then I got my father's 8mm projector, and we watched some black and white triple X movies.

Our gang moved on to grades nine through twelve at Henry P. Becton Regional High School. All the Carlstadt and East Rutherford kids went to school there. The property was donated, and the school was built by Becton, Dickinson and Company, so that was a huge gift to the taxpayers. In my freshman year I signed up for college classes, but I knew the first day that college wasn't for me. The following year I signed up for tech school. In the morning I went to Becton for English, math, history, and gym—then lunch, and off in a bus to Moonachie Technical School for auto body. We smoked pot on the bus to Moonachie School as we rode down Route 17, and on the first day our bus driver, Uncle Al, told us, "Open the windows in the back of the bus, boys!" He wasn't sure of the way to the tech school, so we helped him with directions by taking him through the Lincoln Tunnel into New York City, and we never got to school the first day! Men and women went to the tech school for classes too from neighboring towns of North Arlington, Lyndhurst, Rutherford, East Rutherford, Carlstadt, Woodridge, Hasbrook Heights, and Lodi, so I got to meet a lot of people and became friends with them from all these towns. My mother and father called me "the mayor" because everyone knew me.

Although I was one year in age ahead of my class, I wasn't the first one of us to get my driver's license. Mike Paparella was. His dad owned the property where we had our fort in junior high. In '73, when I was sixteen, crazy Mike "Peppy" was seventeen. One day a fight broke out between Mike and his girlfriend Debbie because Mike wanted to run away to California on his motorcycle, and Debbie wouldn't go with him. Mike's mom and dad didn't want them dating let alone driving to California on his motorcycle, so Mike was furious. He jumped on his bike and gassed it full-throttle down Route 17 on his way to California. Right there across the street from the Crow's Nest restaurant and bar, he crashed his motorcycle and died at the scene. All of us guys were pallbearers at Mike's funeral on what had to be one of the saddest days of our lives. In the limo in front of Saint Joseph's Church, Mike's dad had a heart attack, but he survived.

I turned seventeen in high school, and during that time, I developed a sore throat while on a skiing trip with the school, and spent the next two weeks fighting pneumonia under an oxygen tent in Beth Israel Hospital. During that time a spot was detected on my lung. I had to stay home, rest a lot, and be tutored.

I couldn't go for my driving test, so I studied the written test diligently. When I was released from doctors' care three months later, my father started teaching me to drive in his Big Black Caddy, a 1967, four-door sedan, a beautiful car that I learned to drive well. I passed the written driving test with 100 percent. Driving was no problem. I even parallel parked that boat without hitting the cones, so I got my junior license and was one notch closer to being "the Big Shot."

One Saturday in 1975 during a gas shortage, my friend Jimmy Renke and I were driving the Caddy around looking for a green flag at a gas station because the Caddy was low on gas. We took our eyes off the road for *only two seconds* and smacked into the car in front of us! The Caddy was totaled! We were stunned. The police came and called my dad whose only concern at that moment was if Jimmy and I were okay. The other people were okay too, and the insurance companies paid for the all the damages.

My father wanted to junk the car. I said I could fix it, but he said, "You *can't* fix it!" I argued that I could, so he let me have it. He went out and bought another Caddy, a 1970, four-door sedan. Another boat.

My friend Jimmy and I went looking for parts in junkyards on Saturdays. Finally, in a junkyard in North Arlington on River Road, we found the whole front end of a '67 Caddy nose, a beveled fender, hood, and radiator support—the whole front end! I asked the owner how much for all the pieces, and he wanted only $25. He said that stuff had been taking up too much room, and I was doing him a favor by getting it out of his way. So, we got a truck and brought the parts to my house. My father couldn't believe it!

Me and Jimmy ripped the whole front end off and put the new one on. When I heard an engine tap from the lifters in the motor, I tore the motor down and rebuilt it, too, and, at seventeen, I had my first car, a 1967 black Caddy! All we needed to do was paint the front, so we brought it to my auto body class at Moonachie Tech School where my car became a school project. We stripped and rebuilt the whole car. I put a beautiful black lacquer paint job on it. Then we added some wire-spoked wheels and put big godfather white walls on it. We added some white pin stripes and did the interior in blue velvet. Other additions came—a TV, a bar, and an eight-track player. My first "chick mobile."

High school was the greatest four years of my life! In my junior year, I was driving my big, black "chick mobile" to school. Often I parked in the teachers' parking lot, and over the loud speaker, the principal announced time after time, "Mr. Marakovitz, please move your car!" That ended when my senior year began; the principal called me to his office and told me that he'd arranged a parking space for me during my senior year. I was voted "most popular in my class," and loved that school! Graduation was another big deal at Higgins Field, and we had a huge graduation party at my house. I wanted to go to that school forever. But that didn't happen.

My "chick mobile"

Chapter 3

That's More Like It

AFTER HIGH SCHOOL, I left my father and got a job in a local auto body shop where I was introduced to cocaine. I loved the feeling of being sure I could move mountains. Since turning fifteen, I was definitely on a utopian starship, habitually high with pot, vodka, cocaine, and an endless playing field of women.

My mother worked as a self-taught computer operator in an office with a lot of other women, and I was even messing with my mother's girlfriends who didn't hesitate to party with me. I would get involved with a woman, then leave her for another one. I didn't want to spend the rest of my life with any of them!

I heard that a friend was selling a junk chopper. Even though my mother didn't care for motorcycles, I couldn't resist going after that bike. I bought the chopper and kept it in a garage that I rented for ten dollars a month so my parents wouldn't know about it. After the junk vehicle was torn down and rebuilt completely, it became a stunning blue show chopper.

My friend Chuck was working for my dad then, and one night Chuck and I were out drinking after work. We started talking about when I would show my mom and dad the chopper. I committed to telling them that night when I got home. But, when I got home, I had second thoughts about my mother freaking out about the bike, so I didn't mention it. The next day at work, Chuck asked my dad how he liked my beautiful chopper! You can guess who said this: "Chopper? What chopper? Tony has a chopper?" Chuck wiggled out of the conversation, "He didn't tell you? He was gonna tell you last night."

Dad was waiting for me in the driveway when I got home. He told me to bring the chopper to the house, so, I did. "Wow! What a beautiful bike!" was all he said before calling my mother out of the house to show her what her son had rebuilt. I think they were both in shock. We have a photo of my mom sitting on the chopper. After I'd ridden the bike for a while, a guy offered me far more money than I thought it was worth, so I sold it to him.

Mom trying to adjust

That was the same year I got my tattoo. I'd forgotten about the tattoo until one morning when I woke up after a night of drinking, went to the refrigerator, guzzled some milk out of the carton, and got a blunt reprimand from my mother who saw the tat on my arm and went nuts. "Slim!! He's got a tattoo!!" She screeched my dad's name again, then got up on a chair, and started hitting me on my shoulders with her wooden spoon so hard that she broke the spoon before getting down and running into the bedroom. My mother probably wouldn't have minded the flowers in the body art, but the dagger going through them brought out a side of my mother that I hadn't seen in my lifetime. My dad comforted her, "Honey, he's eighteen now. He can do what he wants." (Thanks, Dad!)

My uninhibited party life rolled on. I'd adopted a lifestyle that I thought was normal. Everybody was doing it, so whatever it was, it was all right, I thought. I remember my father's continual warnings about what happened to my grandmother (alcohol), but I knew better. It didn't stop me from partying in bars like Club Evergreen in Wallington, Dirty Nelly's in Elmwood Park, the Soap Factory in Palisades Park, and Art Stock's Royal Manor in North Brunswick. Sex, drugs, rock and roll, alcohol, and disco were my life. With Wildwood being only three hours from Carlstadt via the Garden State Parkway, my buddies and I took trips there on weekends making great time using a radar detector. The four of us made a game of bouncing quarters off the roof of the car into the change baskets at the toll booths. The guy seated behind the passenger's side was the one who was supposed to bounce the quarters into the baskets. Great fun! My Aunt Paula came along with my family a couple of times. Everyone in the bars thought she was my girlfriend. What a laugh!

In '77 when I was working in the auto body shop at a car dealership in Jersey City, a guy I worked with was getting pills for me. Eventually, I started pushing pills. I was making a lot of money and getting my pills for free. One night I popped too many pills, and my heart felt like it was going to pop right out of my chest. My body heated up—felt like I was on fire! Scared senseless, I ran out of the bar at the place on Second Street in Carlstadt and laid on my back in a pile of snow in the parking lot and said, "God, PLEASE, don't take me!" I lay there for a while and had a one-sided, bargaining conversation with God, promising Him I wouldn't take the pills anymore if He'd let me live. After that night, I stopped taking the pills, but kept selling them for a while because my friends were still doing them, and the money was good. I felt like God answered my prayer before going back to wherever He stayed.

While working at the car dealership, we used to go for lunch—just a couple of sandwiches and beers—at this place by the track called Third Base. It was me, my friend Jimmy, and our boss Charlie. We got to know the owners of Third Base who were opening another bar and restaurant up the road from Third Base called Home Plate. It was "cool" with a huge bar in it shaped like a home plate. They were bringing in live disco, and asked me if I was interested in becoming a head bouncer for them on weekends. What an offer! I accepted immediately and agreed to be there Thursday, Friday, and Saturday nights. I got to be good friends with their son Steve, the manager, who was my age.

All the New York Giants from the stadium used to come in, have dinner, and spend time. My ego swelled even bigger just being there as the head bouncer at the Home Plate with the Giants! I was hanging out with all these men drinking and carrying on. Women were all over the place, and I had my pick. It was crazy. There I met Beverly whose father owned a body shop. He used to fix up wrecks and resell them. I sold my Caddy to my friend Paul Bradley and bought a 1973 Lincoln Mark IV, another chick car! This one even had metallic spoke wheels.

The romance with Beverly went south pretty fast, and I was back to playing the field bouncing at Home Plate and working for my father. At Home Plate I met a car salesman who got me a job in a car dealership in Jersey City. There I met Charlie, Jimmy, and Richie. Eddie was our boss, and Charlie was our manager. That was a crazy time. We were all drug addicts and alcoholics. In the shop, we had a fridge stocked with beer and I.W. Harper Whiskey, something to wash the mescaline down while we worked all day.

At about twenty years into my life, I started hanging out at Dobb's Place and a place on Second Street in Carlstadt, New Jersey, with a group of friends, some from my childhood. We rented ski houses up in Hunter Mountain, New York, from Thanksgiving to Saint. Patrick's Day. A lot of other people would go in it with us for the season. We'd party and ski all weekend. It was a great time of drinking and taking mescaline, a hallucinogenic that kept us high for about six hours.

Then in that year of '79, I went skiing for the weekend at Hunter Mountain, came home, and went straight to a bar called the Finish Line. There I saw her: a beautiful Italian girl with long, black curly hair. Her name was Roseann, and she got my interest. She was single, and we started to date. I was loyal to a woman for the first time in my life. While we were dating, I started to hang out at the Finish Line while she was working. My friends would show up, and the party was ON. One night I was approached by a guy named Dennis who asked if I would be a nighttime manager. I said yes. After dating for about two years, I asked Roseann to marry me. We started saving for a wedding. I worked nights at the Finish Line and days at the car dealership. Then I got approached about dealing cocaine. More money. It was ON. We divided kilos at the wharf in New York, broke it down, cut the kilos into ounces, and sold them for $2,900.00 an ounce. My coke was free. Then I got involved in shylocking and collections. Roseann had no idea what I was doing when I wasn't with her. She didn't know a lot of things.

Chapter 4

That's My Girl

ROSEANN LIVED WITH HER father and her younger sister Suzie in a two-family house that had an apartment upstairs. I never met her mother who died eight years before Roseann and I met. In 1979 Roseann came to my house for Christmas to meet my parents. My mom and aunts loved her like one of their own. They shopped together, hung out together, cooked, and played Yahtzee, and when we announced that we were going to get married, everyone jumped in to help plan Roseann's wedding—dresses, shoes, hair, nails, flowers, bridesmaids, Maid of Honor, Best Man—everyone wanted to be in Roseann's wedding!

We got married on Oct 24,1981, at the Church of the Immaculate Conception in Newark, New Jersey. The reception was nearby at the VFW in Cedar Grove. Ours was a big wedding with two hundred guests. Roseann's sister Gigi was her Maid of Honor, and all her girlfriends were in the wedding party. All my close friends were in the fairytale wedding too. Roseann and I took off for a grand honeymoon in Laguna Beach, California, then to Mexico, then to Universal Studios, Disneyland, and Knott's Berry Farm—lots of sightseeing along the way! It was my first time in California. We came home to start our new life together as Mr. and Mrs. Anthony Joseph Marakovitz! The beginning of our lives together was beautiful. We moved into an apartment above the garage of the house that my parents rented on Hackensack Street where I had lived with my parents, grandfather, and uncle for years. Everyone was happy for us, and we were happy too.

I lost my job at Center Ford because they sold the property and closed the business, so I went back to work with my father and grandfather painting and hanging wall paper. I continued using cocaine and alcohol, but not every day. I was selling cocaine and pot. In 1982 I rented a three-car garage across the street from our home on Hackensack Street in Carlstadt, NJ. My friend Smitty owned a four-family house with the garage in the back that overlooked the NYC skyline. Breathtaking. We used to go back there on a deck that was built next to the shop and watch the Macy's Fourth of July fireworks on the Hudson River.

I worked on antique cars and cars of the 50's, 60's, and 70's, and I loved working on bikes, too. I restored them and put flames on motorcycle tanks, fenders, and bags, too. That was my specialty. I couldn't advertise my underground shop except to give customers t-shirts that said, "Body works by Tony." I employed a full-time mechanic, and we rebuilt motors and did all sorts of mechanical work even with friends who came by and wanted to work with us. We used to make cars disappear that no one wanted to make payments on anymore, so, I guess we did some insurance work too.

The body shop was a party place. When we got shipments of cocaine, a bunch of friends would show up, and a party would break out. Beer and cocaine were easily within reach. We partied and worked all night. Sometimes I'd go for days around the clock partying and working. No neighbors ever complained. Why should they? I worked on their cars too! The neighbors loved me.

After a year and a half, I closed the body shop before I could get in trouble with the I.R.S. Through the workings, I met the CEO of a company through a friend of mine who was at the Finish Line. His girlfriend Irene introduced me to "Poochie" who owned a body shop in Bayonne, New Jersey. Poochie's partner embezzled about a half million dollars, so Poochie removed him and brought me in, giving me an option to buy what was then Ace Body Shop.

Ace was thriving in the beginning. Three guys were working for me towing at a couple of dealerships and a big beverage company, and doing some insurance work. My pay was $500 a week with a 1099. I wanted more money. My cocaine use ramped up and so did the partying. I was never home because I was always with the boys dealing cocaine to make up for the money that I wasn't getting at my real job. Then, the accountant from Poochie's company was assigned to take care of my funds for the shop. He told me he was depositing money in my body shop account, but after he deposited the money, he took half in his own pocket to gamble on horses. Plus, I started to skim money off the top of the dealership's payments to make up the difference in my pay. It wasn't long before the accountant got caught, and he almost took me out with him.

In the meantime, I was in a bad motorcycle accident. I broke my collarbone, had severe road rash on my arms and legs, and suffered a serious concussion after my helmet broke and flew off my head. Roseann nurtured me back to health. For six months, I had to sleep wearing a back brace while sitting up in the living room.

When I finally got back to the shop in 1984, all hell broke loose. The accountant took all the charges, and I skated from prosecution. That had to be God, but at the time, I didn't know it. My partying was going strong. Roseann didn't know how much partying I was doing and how crazy my life was. I had no idea that I was becoming an addict of all sorts. I thought I was living a normal life because everyone I knew was doing what I was doing, except Roseann. She was always with my mom and aunts while I was riding down every new path of destruction.

Another job came along from a friend who worked as an auto insurance adjuster for a well-known, national company. The company chose me to be on the anti-theft team. If they thought a claim was bogus, they would send me on the claim to see if it was real or a scam. I was in a drive-in claims center in Jersey City, New Jersey. Do you know there is no other Jersey City anywhere in the world? Cars that had been in accidents would come in for insurance claims on side swipes, broken lights, and so forth—mostly the cars were drivable. With this job, I could go on the road. Furthermore,

I was bonded to write out checks to the insured, if I thought the claim was legit.

It wasn't long before I was connected with a body shop that was conveniently next to the drive-in claim office. Soon I was back dealing cocaine and hot cars. I could write a check from the insurance company and bring the people to the auto body shop practically next door to work on their cars. Then, I'd collect the checks I wrote to them for the work.

Roseann and I separated for a while, and I moved in with a girl named Laurie. There was nothing between us. She was in one room, and I was in another. She needed help with her rent, so I paid her in cocaine. What a deal! That didn't last too long. I moved out, reconciled with Roseann, and moved back into our place.

Eventually I was asked to resign from the insurance company because of missing days, smelling like alcohol, and being high at work. I didn't care. I was making plenty of money working at the auto body shop with hot cars, and drug dealing was brisk. That came to an end because I became the head bouncer at my father's friend's bar, Shakers, one of the hottest clubs near Giants Stadium in Carlstadt, New Jersey. I worked double shifts from 11 a.m. 'til 2 a.m., and I'd walk out with $700 a day, plus my cocaine business was moving. On weekends I worked in an after-hours, multi-level club in NYC on 54th Street between Second and First Streets that was owned by the family. Upstairs was a VIP room where anything happened—orgies, drugs, etc. There I was, the Bouncer with a Big .45 sticking out of my jacket.

I was also the Dealer. Cocaine, of course. The first floor of the after-hours club was all gambling—blackjack, craps, the money wheel, poker tables—it was all there from Friday after midnight until Monday morning at six o'clock. I used to bring a bunch of dancers from Shakers to the after-hours club. The cops never busted the club. They were on the payroll.

I always believed in God. I just didn't know Him at all. If anyone was nice to me, I thought she was an angel. I thought angels kept me from harm. I thought if I went to Hell, all my friends would be there. I didn't know that friendship and love come from

God, and that friends aren't found in Hell, but that makes sense. I didn't know a lot of things. I didn't know up from down, but I thought I knew everything.

I met a long-time friend named Billy who worked for a national beer distributor, and he started bouncing with me at Shakers. His father was a shop steward for the union at the beer company, so Billy offered to talk with him about getting me a job. I got on a temp list there, and they called me when they needed me.

Billy's sister was getting married, so Billy and two other guys and I went to a bachelor party for Billy's brother-in-law to be. It was pure fun being with those guys until we got pulled over by a cop who cited me for a broken tail light on Route 17. Not only that, he smelled alcohol on all of us, but since I was driving, I was the one who had to take the roadside sobriety test. I refused the breathalyzer and took the consequences of being arrested and having my car impounded. The guys had to find their own way to the bachelor party while I went to jail until 5 o'clock in the morning when the cop asked me if there was anyone I could call for a ride home. The answer was obvious. Nice of him to drive me home.

Without a license, I couldn't, of course, drive the beer truck, but it got worse. The court took my license away for six months and ordered me to go to a DUI class in Paramus, New Jersey, about a half hour from home. Things worked out, though. The CEO of the beer distributor let me keep my job, not as a driver, but as a guy who rode along to load and unload the beer. The DUI school was at four o'clock on the way home from the route, so the beer truck dropped me off at the school, and Roseann came and picked me up after the class. Three weeks went by, and, by some quirk, I was allowed to leave the school.

After about six months at Shakers, I left to do temp work for the beer distributor, and on the days when I wasn't called, I worked with my father. At that time there was no drug testing; all that was required was a valid driver's license to be hired as a temp to drive a two-man, eight-bay truck. Every morning drivers would get their routes and loads, then go from bar to bar and liquor store to liquor store delivering beer. It was awesome. The base pay was

$125. Then the driver got a quarter cost of every case delivered. So, if a driver delivered 900 cases and 16 kegs, he would get $225 for the cases, $48 for the kegs, plus $125 base pay, totaling $398 for about four hours of work before coming back in and going out on a second load. It varied. Once I got my CDL, I could drive a sixteen-bay tractor trailer that held 1600 cases, so the money started to flow even bigger for me. Plus, I was still dealing cocaine and pot. Roseann and I were still married. I couldn't have told you anything about our wedding vows. I wouldn't have remembered promising anything to her or to God. I was busy having fun with my guy friends and other women. I didn't need anyone else or anything else, especially money.

Chapter 5

That's The Way I Like It

WHAT PEOPLE WON'T DO for love, money, or fun! I thought I had seen it all, but in 1989 I ran into a friend who used to have a juice bar with exotic dancers—actually nothing more than fervent strippers. My friends and I brought vodka there for fun. I met this friend again at the old Finish Line Bar where I'd met Roseann ten years before that. He and his dad who grew up with my dad were opening a strip club called First and Ten, so I helped them set up and became the bouncer at night. I delivered beer during the day and worked there for a while during the week. In 1990, this guy and his dad opened an amazing sports bar with about eighty-five TV screens throughout the place, and I worked Security there on weekends while I delivered beer during the week. What a cool place! Lots of sports figures hung out there, especially on Sundays during football season. If the New York Giants played at home, there were lines to get into the place! The ball players had their own VIP room upstairs, and I would stand on the staircase with a clipboard full of names sorting out who could go to the VIP room. What a great time! Partying all the time was my style! Everyone was doing it, so it was normal for me. At that time, I could always hold my own. If I had just the right amount of cocaine and vodka, I knew everything that was going on around me and every woman who passed by.

One night in the sports bar, I noticed a girl who kept staring at me. She showed up every weekend, and when she was staring, I'd move to a different post with my radio contact that was linked to twenty-two other guys who were off-duty state police, DEA agents, and local moonlighting police. Without fail, the girl would move to where I was. When I asked her if she was following me, she said she was, and asked me if I would have a drink with her. I signed off my post. She, Barbara, knew I was married, but that didn't stop either one of us. We were both living to party.

Barbara had been living in a house with her boyfriend in Nyack, New York. He wasn't around that night, so that gave us a place and a routine excuse that seemed to work even after I dragged into home the next morning. We didn't have cell phones then, so communication was extremely limited. A lot happened then that couldn't happen these days! During that time my grandfather passed away, but I was so wasted day and night that I barely remember the wake or the funeral. Life was a blur at eye level.

One night Roseann got locked out of our house, so my father drove her to the bar where I was working in order to get my keys. I saw my dad's work van pull into the parking lot behind me when I was in my car about to leave with Barbara. When Roseann told me that she came to get the house keys and asked, "Who is she?" I lied telling her Barbara was some girl that I was trying to help because she needed a ride. Roseann was mortified. So was my dad. They knew I was lying. I gave Roseann the keys and said I'd see her at home, but I didn't go home until the next day. Roseann wasn't there. Not long after that, Roseann found a card from Barbara in the glovebox in my car. What did it say? It was a "Thinking about you . . . Love you forever" card. It was clear to Roseann that Barbara was more than just a friend.

My next move was back into my mom and dad's apartment on River Road in nearby Lyndhurst. At thirty-three years old, my messed-up self had to move back with my parents! As fast as I was making money, I was blowing it on partying and being a big shot. Sadly, I couldn't take basic care of myself. I took better care of my cars.

After work one night I came home tired. My mother made dinner, and after that, I went upstairs to bed. Unprecedented. Around midnight my father came busting through the door yelling that my mother was dead! We ran into their bedroom. He grabbed her and shook her, gasping, "Look! She's DEAD!" No response from what looked like a blue-faced ragdoll. My dad was crying frantically and tearing his hair out, and when I saw his hysteria, something I'd never felt before washed over me. It was a sensation of calmness, even in my voice, as I spoke, "Dad, call 911, open the doors to the house, and leave me alone with her, okay?"

I lifted my mom off the bed, gently settled her on the carpeted floor, and with the presence of mind to tilt her head back, I started doing CPR from what I could remember seeing on TV—rhythmic chest compressions followed by two quick breaths. Just as she appeared to be coming back, I'd lose her again! Where were the paramedics!? Suddenly, I heard the ambulance, and the sound of paramedics coming up the stairs! They jolted my mother with defibrillator paddles, lifted her onto a gurney, and, moments later, sped off with her to the hospital in Passaic.

Dad and I left the hospital when she finally stabilized in the middle of the night, but were back there the next morning to see her looking fine—like nothing ever happened the night before! She was ready to come home, but the doctor wanted to keep her in the hospital for about a week for tests and rest. Everyone came to visit her. Her room was full of get-well cards, flowers, and gifts. People loved my mother and knew that life without her wouldn't be nice at all.

On the morning after her heart attack, my mother expressed an urgency to talk to me. She wanted to know what I was doing on top of her in the middle of the night. She said she remembered me taking her off the bed and placing her on the floor. She said she was hovering in the corner of the ceiling at that time, but couldn't see what I was doing, and she went on to say that she saw Jesus with my grandmother. Apparently, Jesus was waving for my mother to come toward Him, but my grandmother was shouting at her, "Go back! Go back! You need to take care of Anthony!"

This overwhelmed me. I was sure God had been in the room with me and my father and the paramedics and who knows who else? My dad couldn't believe that she was alive, talking, back to normal, and ready to go home. He cried when the doctor told him that I saved her life. Seriously, it was a miracle that I was even home and functioning at all. My mother taught me to run to God and to never blame Him for things that don't go our way because He is always there. He must've been there that night, but I didn't take notice of him. After we got home, I took my fried brains back to work. That was that.

I was still living at home in 1991when the Giants beat the Buffalo Bills and won the Super Bowl. Channel 7 Eyewitness News was at the sports bar celebration interviewing the players. I was still there working Security, so I was on the news! When the season ended, the sports bar closed, and things changed again.

The next year, Barbara and I met some friends who took over a multi-level bar on the Hudson River. This place rocked all week! There was Reggae at a tiki-bar and restaurant outside downstairs and a rock band at the club upstairs. I became head of Security, hiring off-duty police officers. Barbara became head of the waitresses. We opened for lunch and closed at 4 a.m. There were docks for boats. It wasn't long before I had to supply Security for 1,000 boats in the marina! Yes, we were rockin'! And, too, it wasn't long before one of the owners and I got into dealing cocaine at the club. I was distributing beer during the day and working Security during nights at the club with Barbara.

One night when Barbara and I were hanging out at the bar, I had my arm around her and we were kissing, when I heard, "Oh, God. There's Joe—over there by the door, and he's watching us!" Barbara had a young daughter with her first husband, a different guy also named Joe who owned a successful trucking company. They shared custody of their little girl when she and Joe divorced. She divorced her second husband, too. This Joe at the door was only a boyfriend, a wealthy CPA who had been sharing his life and home with Barbara for about five years. Barbara said she was thinking of leaving him anyway, so, once Joe was out of the

31

scenario, Barbara and I rented a second-floor condo together on the Hudson River by the Tappan Zee Bridge. The boyfriend Joe seemed like a nice person. He gave Barbara a car and some furniture, so we were set.

In time I lost my job with the beer distributor for missing too many days, but I was making lots of money at the club at the marina. Lots of money! A thousand dollars a week— then, on weekends we collected a cover charge, and the money was really rolling in! Figure it: 600 people at ten dollars each was all gravy! So, of course, I started skimming money off the top. I was a big shot having fun with the wrong crowd, heading in the wrong direction fast.

Throughout the summer, I sometimes stayed on a forty-foot yacht in the marina because the bar closed at 4 a.m. Barbara would go home, and I would sleep on the boat because I had to get up early to open the restaurant early. The yacht belonged to one of my friend's girlfriends who was a cocaine dealer and part owner of the bar. The yacht was stocked with Dom Perignon, champagne, wine, and beer, and it was a convenient place for me to shower, keep my clothes for work, and even cheat on Barbara when the opportunity often presented itself until the bar closed at the end of the season.

My mother and dad were beyond devastated when Roseann and I separated, and, of course, Barbara wasn't welcome in my mother's house, even at Christmastime, so I stayed in Nyack in the condo that Barbara and I rented together. In the winter of 1992, I was out of a job after the season closed, so I went back to work during the days for my father. Barbara was waitressing in a mall restaurant in Nyack. While she was working at night, I was out partying. I'd pick Barbara up at the end of her shift, and we'd go out to have fun carrying on like drunks.

I learned one night that my friend Mike had a bad accident. He was a single guy from Indiana with no family, so I went to see him in the hospital. Turns out he got drunk the night before and went home without his keys. He ignored any thoughts of danger while shimmying up a pole to the second floor of his house and walking across the roof to the bedroom window. Once there, he tried to lift the window, but instead he put his arm through the glass and severed an artery near his wrist. Blood shot all over the room! He managed to call 911 and walked down the stairs to the outside to wait for help. The paramedics found him collapsed and bleeding profusely in the middle of the street. He nearly lost his life! He was a hard-working, smart guy, the general manager of a popular restaurant chain. He traveled across Long Island, New York, spending a year at each new store. His job was to hire all the help and raise up general managers. He'd been doing this for seventeen years and was good at it. Mike's desire was to get his own restaurant in Indiana and stay there after his final assignment in Nyack. His request was granted by the company. That year Mike and I hung out with Barbara and our friends and the employees at the restaurant.

In the meantime, I moved on from working for my father and started working for Aunt Paula at her stone company, setting tombstones on graves. I drove a huge truck with a crane and placed headstones, some weighing a thousand pounds or more, at gravesites. Then I got involved in tiling floors and picking up slabs of granite and marble for fabricating kitchen counter tops, vanities, and fireplace surrounds.

In 1995 Mike was ready to move back to Indiana. The company gave him a moving truck and hired me to drive. I took a two-week vacation from my Aunt Paula's company to help Mike move from Nyack to Anderson, Indiana. We linked his car to the tow hitch and drove high on cocaine most of the way to his new restaurant located next door to a strip club. Who could make this up? We became quick friends with the owner and spent time with him and the strippers in Mike's new apartment after the place closed until daylight. I was married to alcohol, seriously engaged to cocaine, and on my way back to Nyack to work for my aunt the next day. And, oh, yeah, to Barbara.

Barbara wasn't as happy to see me as I expected. She was an angry drunk, and so was I, and it wasn't long before the neighbors in our condo were calling the police because the sound of our fighting rattled the walls all the way down the hallways. One of us was about to be arrested for domestic violence, and I was the one to go first because the rule of thumb with the police is to take the man if they can't decide who did what. I wasn't in the jail cell for long, though. An hour later, they arrested Barbara because she beat up an officer after they took me away. She spent the night in jail for assaulting the officer, but because her brother-in-law was a judge in Nyack, she got off!

So, that was that for Barbara and me. I waited for her to go to work on the weekend. Then my father and Aunt Paula helped me load up a truck full of my stuff so I could move back to my parents' apartment in Lyndhurst.

Was I still married to Roseann? Of course. Why not? At least that's what I thought, but Roseann got in touch with me to tell me that before her father passed away, he left her some money for her to divorce me. She left me a knife and fork on the table. Oh, yes, and a waterbed. My family had waited in vain for fourteen years to have grandchildren.

So, in 1994 Barbara and I split up, Roseann divorced me, and I was living in my parents' apartment and working with Aunt Paula in the granite business. I worked hard all year, then I'd fly out to Indiana to go to the Indy 500 with Mike twice a year. His friend Big George would get us police escorts to the track, and we'd be partying up a storm all week before the race. I can't remember the go-go stripper's name that I was so fond of, but she followed me back to New Jersey for a month or so to dance at my friends' clubs. I saw myself as a successful playboy, a high-class, movie-worthy, big spender who loved the idea of buying rounds for all my laughing, drinking friends. I drank in the mornings to get rid of the shakes for the next twenty years. Much of my time was spent with high school friends, partying wherever a party was happening.

Chapter 6

Lovin' the Limelight

I TOOK NOTICE OF a beautiful woman named Michole at Jake's Place one Friday night. I was buying her drinks because she told me that she broke up with her boyfriend. We wound up at that tiki bar where I used to work with Barbara and stayed there 'til closing at 4 a.m. After watching the sunrise at a private beach with a good amount of cocaine and beer, we went to her place in Nutley for breakfast. Michole, divorced with no children, was an executive saleswoman for a national phone company, and soon I moved in with her. There were benefits beyond just having a nicer place to stay. One night Michole came home from work with a gift-wrapped box for me. I opened it and pulled out a cell phone. "Now, I'll be able to call you and know where you are whenever I need you," she told me. Wow! I needed something like this, and, to makes things even better, it was a company cell phone on a family package, paid for by her company!

We had a lot of friends who were couples who loved to go with us to a great Brazilian rodizio grill in Newark where the waiters would walk around with skewers of steak, pork, sausage, etc. and the menu was an all-you-can-eat deal for $19.95! Us guys would hang outside the restaurant before dinner, smoking pot and getting good 'n hungry before finding our table with the women. After filling up with food and plenty of sangria, we'd go to Jake's

Place for the entertainment where this guy named Frosty would show up with a keyboard and a trumpet.

One night I talked with him and told him I played drums. Frosty invited me to bring the drums to jam with him, so I called my godfather, Joey Cass, and asked him if he had any drums for sale. He had a beautiful Ludwig set with amazing Zildjian cymbals. The best! I took them to the bar and jammed with Frosty playing great stuff that everybody liked. We clicked, and at that time in my life, I felt awesome playing music again. Before long, I was playing drums in the bars in Carlstadt with Frosty. A big banner outside a huge banquet hall advertised us, "Frostbite Featuring Tony Marakovitz on Drums." We were a huge draw. Everyone came, even people from grammar school. I was high on cocaine, vodka, and life with all my friends there, a beautiful woman for my girlfriend, and being in the limelight playing music that made everything come alive beyond alive! Life was good!

In May of that year, about fifteen of us flew to Indiana for the Indy 500 for five days. We stayed at Mike's house and in Big George's condo. What a blast that was! On our way home, I got past airport security with the cocaine that I had stuffed in my underwear. Michole lost our tickets to fly, so we were in the airport about four hours early. While I was standing there, I saw John Walsh from *America's Most Wanted*, the TV program that found tough criminals on the run. My friend Jamie bet me $100 that the man was *not* John Walsh, so we walked over, and, sure enough, the man *was* John Walsh at the Indy Five Hundred! John Walsh shook my hand, and we talked for a few minutes. John asked if we had a video camera, so Jamie pulled his camera out and started recording me with John Walsh. Then John called Michole to stand between us and announced, "I'm John Walsh. This is *America's Most Wanted*, and I'm standing here with Tony and his wife. Tony is married to three women at the same time! That's *America's Most Wanted*, and you're busted! Now snap the cuffs on him!" he joked. By this time there was a crowd around us, and everyone was laughing. It was cool. John Walsh was a wonderful man with a great sense of humor.

I was back to working with my father because Aunt Paula had to let me go for not showing up or for showing up too high to work. I was high all the time and thought that was normal. My parents accepted Michole, and we went with them to my Uncle Rocky's condo in Myrtle Beach for two weeks in 1997, the same year that Michole told me she was pregnant. She stopped drinking and drugging for those nine months, but I didn't.

Michole and I were married in January, 1998, at the Harvest Moon restaurant off Route 17 in Sloatsburg, NY. My friend Chuck who owned the restaurant knew the mayor who officiated. About 100 people, including Michole's two brothers, her aunts, uncles, and our friends were there for the wedding and dinner. Our parents were thrilled to know that their first grandchild would be born that year. Our families bonded right away. We had a beautiful wedding, and postponed our honeymoon until after our baby was born.

There were a lot of good memories in the house Michole and I rented in Carlstadt when Holly was born because it was the house of my childhood friend Chuck Routar! Years before that, when his parents went on vacation and left him at home, I moved in with him, and we did some serious partying. This house is where Michole, Holly, and I settled for a while. I went back to work.

At a very early stage of Michole's pregnancy, we got a phone call from her doctor telling us that Michole not only had Hepatitis C, but also was HIV-positive. I was neither. This news meant our baby would require attentive prenatal care and special birth procedures at the Newark University Hospital. By attentive, I mean, Michole and I had to enroll in a trial study at the hospital to educate ourselves about Hepatitis C and HIV. For a year I had to inject medication into Michole's hip to cure the Hepatitis, and Michole had to drink a medicinal cocktail for the HIV. Our beautiful daughter Holly arrived on June 25, 1998, completely healthy. A miracle.

Michole's parents took care of Holly while Michole and I took our honeymoon trip to a beach resort in Aruba. At the airport in Aruba, I handed a hundred-dollar bill to a guy who was working there and asked him where the *yayo* was. He came back with some good Jamaican weed and cocaine that kept us flying for the whole time we were there. In fact, because we couldn't take that Jamaican rocket fuel back with us, we gave it to a guy at a bar who would've paid us whatever we asked for it!

Michole didn't want any crosses on the walls of our rented house in Carlstadt because she and her parents were Jewish. Even so, they got along well with my parents. In fact, they drove from Philly to spend a real Holly-jolly Christmas and Hannukah with us in Carlstadt. My mother made the traditional seven-fish Christmas Eve dinner with all our family and Michole's family. We woke Holly up at midnight to see what Santa brought her. Our little girl got presents every day for Hannukah, too, plus dunes of presents that were under our tree like what I got when I was a baby. Our families came together for birthdays, barbeques, holidays, and for no other reason than to just be together. But life was still all about me. At forty years old, I was still Mr. Big Stuff—high all the time, drinking, drugging, and cheating on my wife, daughter, and family.

I went back to work for my Aunt Paula's company again doing granite counter tops and fireplace surrounds and setting up tombstones. I worked seventy-five to ninety hours a week and was making good money in 1998. For Holly's first birthday we had a big barbeque at our house for about a hundred fifty friends, family, and neighbors. We set up our band, Frostbite, starring me on the drums. We played for about three hours. What a great day!

As Holly got older, our parents took turns spoiling her on weekends, bringing her back on Sunday nights. Michole and I would hang out at Jake's Place in Lyndhurst where I played the drums with Frostbite on Fridays. Then our friends would come to our house partying with cocaine, pot, and booze 'til the sun came up the next morning. We were straight when Holly was home. I'd get up and go to work after having a couple of vodkas before leaving the house.

In the year 2000, my friend Chuck gave us the news that he wanted us to move because his daughter was getting married and needed a place. It was only right, but at the time, I wasn't happy about it. I was in full addiction and couldn't handle anything.

One night I took a twenty-five-minute drive to New York in our new Jeep Cherokee to score some cocaine. I remember driving toward the Lincoln Tunnel. The next thing I knew, I woke up in the middle of a grassy patch in front of a bridge truss. In the distance I could see cars flying in both directions. Somehow, I got back on the highway westbound and got home. The next thing that woke me up was my wife yelling, "What happened to the Jeep!?" I didn't know. She told me that the side of the Jeep was covered with grass, and the two tires on the driver's side were flat! She was right. I spent most of that day cleaning the Jeep, buying and replacing two tires and rims with the help of a friend who worked at a Jeep store. Then I went back to see if I could figure out what happened. It was raining that night. I saw where I drove between two telephone poles, barely missing them, before spinning out and stopping. I don't remember driving home. God must've been with me that night and even before that night with the way I was living. That I was still alive *had* to be a miracle!

Michole wanted me to quit my job at my aunt's company in 2000 because I was never home and was always partying high while I was working. So, I quit, which wasn't easy because my boss couldn't get anyone else to do my job. He offered me big bucks to reconsider, but I turned down his offer.

In the summer of 2000, we bought a beautiful house in Lynd-hurst right around the block from my parents. The two-story house had three bedrooms, a one-car garage, a new kitchen, a finished basement (my man cave), and a finished attic, a great place for me to unwind with my drums. In the backyard was a pool for Holly.

I got a job with a landscaping company owned by a friend who used to have a sports bar and a strip club. He hired me as a driver with a crew of four other guys to cut grass, spread mulch, and design landscaping. This seemed like fun. All along I was fighting my addiction hard. As soon as I got up in the morning, I'd have my vodkas before I went to work because I couldn't drink during the day. At the end of the day, the guys would go to the bar, pick up a few ounces of cocaine, and put away a couple of drinks before going home. That's the path I chose while trying to be a father to my daughter and a husband to my wife who *knew* when I was partying. I couldn't shake the addiction. I wanted to, but I didn't have a clue how to stop, so I kept going, numb to my own feelings and to my family's feelings, and tramping deeper into denial. It didn't even occur to me that I was hurting my daughter and my wife by favoring drugs and alcohol over them.

At first I thought I was seeing a small plane from the New Jersey side of the Hudson River heading toward the side of the Twin Towers. I was watching from a distance that day and thought how strange the big fire looked in the distance. I was in my truck trying to figure out what was happening when word came over my radio that a jet had hit one of the Twin Towers! I watched the second jet hit! From a distance it looked like a rocket! I heard on the radio that New York was under attack, so I sped to Holly's preschool and went straight home to find Michole and my parents. Our house was in the path of Newark's airport. Normally planes flew over our house to land, and jets would take off nearby, but on that day, there was an unfamiliar sound in the air. Only fighter jets!

Details of the September 11th attack started to untangle about the hijacked planes—who was behind the attacks, the jet that crashed in Pennsylvania, and the one that hit the Pentagon. The New York skyline would never be the same. We had watched the Towers being built and were seeing them come down amid a monstrous, menacing plume of toxic smoke and flying debris that could be seen, we found out later, from space. The damage to human life, the environment, and property was staggering. We got out of town. Michole and I rented a van and headed for Myrtle Beach, South Carolina, with Holly and my parents for two weeks. We had New York plates on our van, and all the way to Myrtle Beach, drivers honked their horns to show their support for America's extraordinary ability to rally and overcome!

Chapter 7

That's Not What I Thought Would Happen

IN 2001 I BOUGHT my friend's landscaping company complete with residential and commercial customers, two trucks, a salter for winter plows, a trailer filled with two mowers, weed whackers, edgers, and blowers. Five workers stayed with me, and we started out okay.

It didn't take long for my routine to change. I would drop off Holly at school, pick up the workers, then drop them off at about ten different jobs in the same location. I'd leave the trailer with the workers in order to free myself up to meet my drug dealer at a bar in the morning. I'd drive back to the work site at noon to bring lunch to the guys and to make sure they did all the work. We'd have lunch together, then we'd go to the next set of jobs. I'd drop them off, set them up, and go to a girl's house to do some cocaine. I'd be on time to pick up Holly from school and bring her home. Someone, either Michole's mom or mine, would be there for her, so I thought I was being a good father and husband. I lied to everyone, even myself.

In 2002 I started losing customers fast because they became wise to my addictions and careless behavior. I couldn't make the insurance payments or the payroll, and couldn't pay to repair equipment, so I had to close the landscaping business. Michole's brother was a CPA who did the paperwork to keep our taxes in line, so we didn't have to declare bankruptcy. I wanted to start up the landscaping again, but that didn't happen.

While hanging at my friend's bar and selling cocaine in Lyndhurst, I met two guys who were dispatchers for a trucking company that delivered mattresses in New Jersey, New York state, and Philadelphia. I still had my CDL from the beer company, so I filled out an application to work with these guys. I failed the drug test, but the company gave me a week to clean up—in other words, no cocaine for a week—and another chance to take the drug test. I passed the second time and was soon driving a tractor trailer loaded with mattresses to all destinations. I felt that God was giving me another chance!

My dad and I were shattered when we heard that my mom was diagnosed with lung cancer. It was bad. She started chemo right away at Passaic General Hospital, and at the same time, my father started treatment for diabetes in the University Hospital in Newark, New Jersey. Michole and I were running from one hospital to the other until my mother and dad finally came home after nursing care was set up for both of them. Sometimes things started to look up. My mom and dad always said, "When the chips are down, pray!" so that's what we did. We desperately needed miracles. My mom was going through chemo, and my dad was taking antibiotics to try to beat an infection in his toes and feet so they wouldn't have to be amputated. I was praying and using drugs and alcohol at the same time to kill the pain from what was happening to them. My addiction was bad, and seeing my mother and dad suffering took me right over the edge! My mom lost all her hair. Aunt Paula was helping as much as she could, even buying wigs for my mother. I went back to driving for the trucking company and trying to stay sober, but that wasn't working. I, too, was getting sicker by the day.

Michole was supportive at that time. Holly was five and knew that my parents were both ill. When Holly visited them with Michole and me, that little girl could pour out joy on my mom and dad like no one else could! Their eyes glowed, and they would forget their pain when Holly was near them.

By September 2002, my mom was finished with chemo, and my father seemed to bounce back, so we thought about going to South Carolina for a short vacation; however, the doctors didn't want my mom to travel. We got through Thanksgiving and Christmas and into 2003. We prayed for a new year of miracles for my parents.

In 2003 my mother developed brain tumors, and my dad's toes started to turn black again. He had to go for an hour of intravenous antibiotics every day as an outpatient in Clifton, New Jersey, a fifteen-minute ride from the house. My Aunt Paula took him for the treatments or I would go into work late after taking him there. The treatments worked! The infection cleared up after a month. Then, he developed a pain in his back from a staph infection on his spine and had to undergo a serious operation that sent him into rehab to learn to walk again, but he never did. He was confined to a wheelchair. Seeing my dad, a man who had always been so outgoing, climbing ladders effortlessly, now struggling to get around in a wheelchair, blew me away. Before long he and my mother were side-by-side in hospice! What a turn of events! I drank a lot and smoked pot before I could visit them. I was a husband and father, high and buzzed up, going to see my mother and father with my family. How sick is that? I thought the booze and pot would ease my pain when I saw them, but it didn't.

At work I was drinking and getting high while driving a tractor trailer, delivering mattresses all over NYC and NY State, New Jersey, and Philly—not being there for my family as a father, husband, or son. I couldn't support anyone. Not even myself. It was then, on July 29, 2003, that I was drinking and getting high in a bar when my cell phone rang. My father wanted to talk with me. "Son, your mother has left us."

Michole had just returned from a thirty-day rehab program. She had decided to do something about her own drinking, so, after the rehab, she was not drinking anymore. I called her, and she got a sitter for Holly so we could be with my dad. Michole was tolerating my drinking because of what I was going through. That night, after we spent time with my father, we went out to eat, and I continued to drink beers and Glenlivet whiskey on the rocks. We went home to try to get some sleep.

The next day I went to work for a half day then went with Aunt Paula and Uncle Jimmy to the funeral home to arrange the wake and funeral. I don't remember my mother's wake because I drank and drugged my way through it. I had cocaine on me and a vial of vodka in my jacket, plus a gallon of vodka in the car for refilling the vial. I have no recollection of this ever happening, but people told me that I jumped on my mother's coffin and almost knocked it over during the wake. Early the next day I was already high and drunk and ready to go to the funeral to say goodbye to my mother. The funeral procession drove through our neighborhood passing my mother's house on the way to the cemetery. A big part of me was buried that day; my mother was always my best friend.

You might know the term reception, but our family called it a "repass." This follows the funeral when family and friends meet to talk and eat together in an informal setting to offer condolences and share memories of the departed loved one. We met in the New Park Tavern in East Rutherford to do this before taking my father back to hospice. I see now that God gave my father the strength to make it through those two days. Watching my mother and father dying together nearly killed me as well. My father was alone in hospice in the very room he shared with the love of his life, my mom.

Dad came to our house for a Sunday dinner after that, and we stopped by the cemetery along the way to spend a few moments at my mother's gravesite. My mother's death was still tender to all of us. Michole, Holly, and I walked across the grass to a restroom in the cemetery's office because Holly wanted to use the restroom. As I waited outside, the sight of my father beside my mother's grave became a freeze frame in my head that still causes me to weep. There, all alone, was my feeble, shaky Dad, who couldn't even manage his own wheelchair; yet, he had been helping me paint our new house less than one year before then!

My Aunt Paula got a hold of me to help her clear out my mother and father's apartment. She gave away almost everything they owned to people who needed furniture, pots and pans, beds, appliances, etc. My mom and dad's personal belongings ended up at my house. I was messed up that day, too—so messed up that I never stopped long enough to have a hangover. Michole didn't want me in our bed anymore. I slept on the couch downstairs if I made it home. My routine was driving the truck for the mattress company, going to the bar, drinking, doing cocaine, going home when the bar closed at 2 a.m. to sleep on the sofa. I can't remember if I saw my daughter and wife. Those days are a blur to me, but I do remember asking God to show me what was happening, even though I don't remember hearing anything from Him.

A change came on Saturday, September 27, 2003. Michole and Holly went to Philly for the weekend, and I was supposed to be working. I don't remember working that day, but I remember driving to Haverstraw, New York, and partying all night. The next thing I remember is waking up on a Sunday in my car at about six o'clock in the morning in front of our house with my wife and Holly standing by the door watching me pull into our driveway, hitting Michole's parked car, then stumbling out of my car. Michole had to go to work. I was supposed to watch Holly, but, instead, Holly was going to work with Michole that day. That was okay with me. I slept on the couch all day and woke up around five o'clock. Michole was outside with our friends and Holly. I walked outside to say hello to everyone, and Michole said, in front of everyone, that she was calling the cops to get me out of the house. She went inside to call 911 on our wall phone, and I tried to stop her by smacking the phone out of her hand. The phone broke!

Obviously, Michole had had enough of me. When she went outside to use her cell phone, I said to our friends, "Let's get in the car and leave!" But, as I got in the car to leave with my friend Flash and his wife, the cops pulled up and ordered me to stay in the car and for Flash to drive me to the police station. At the station Holly and Michole were in one room, and I was in another where I was told to sign a restraining order or be arrested on a domestic violence charge. I signed it and asked to see Holly. Holly and I hugged and kissed, and I told her not to worry because I'd be back home soon, but I was wrong. The police drove me back to my house and gave me a half hour to get my stuff. Still thinking this would all blow over in a couple of days and I'd be back home, I took a small suitcase with some clothes. In the meantime, the police were busy confiscating my gun collection in my mancave! They took my 7mm German sniper rifle from WW II, a couple of replicas of Bat Masterson and Wyatt Earp pistols, and five hundred knives encased in glass for show! They told me they were taking the whole collection because I might use one of the weapons on my wife! I argued that I'd go to the kitchen for a knife if I wanted to do that! That was the last time I saw my prized stockpile. Somebody somewhere else cashed in on all my stuff! I had nowhere to put it anyway. I was on my way to staying with my friend Flash and his wife that day. On the way, I stopped at a bar for some booze and cocaine to lull myself into a stupor. My excuse was to kill the pain of my mother dying, my father in hospice, and my getting thrown out of my house with a restraining order. I woke up in my friend's basement the next morning and called in sick at work.

My friend Flash went to work. His wife was in the kitchen. When she saw the bottle of Scotch I brought up from the basement, she said, "You're drinking already? You have to go to work." She didn't like hearing that I'd taken the day off, so she asked me to take her to where Flash was working to bring him lunch. Flash got nervous when he saw how messed up I was, so his wife stayed at the garage where he was working as a mechanic, and I left.

I drove by my house where I saw Michole standing outside. She saw me passing, driving around the corner, and parking where I could see the house. The guy who was there, I found out later, was a locksmith changing all the locks. While I sat there in my car, a police car stopped in front of me. The officer wanted to report me for breaking the restraining order. I pulled away, but the officer spotted me doing a U-turn. He came after me and arrested me for being less than 500 feet from the house. I was on my way to jail where I was tested for alcohol and was slapped with a DUI. I sprang out the next day after posting bail.

I woke up at my friend's house again. I had passed out and was awakened by the police that afternoon who took me to a hospital for observation. My friend wanted to help me, so I checked out of the hospital and went back to his house where he told me I had to leave. My Aunt Paula put me up in a hotel for a night, and the next day I went back to driving a truck again. I got a room in what was previously an old boarding house above my friend's bar for $75 a week. The bathroom was down the hall.

My wife Michole was visiting my father in hospice and telling him everything she knew that was going on between us. My father was telling me that Michole didn't want me anymore. I was working and partying every night convincing myself that I was doing this to kill my pain, and I stopped going to see my father. The month of October flew by. I wanted to end my life. I just didn't want to live anymore. I ordered another round one night in a place where I went two or three times a week, and I got served with twenty days to respond to a petition for child support! I represented myself in court because I couldn't afford a lawyer, and the judge hit me with paying $450 a week!

At the end of October, I'd had enough. I took enough oxycodone, I thought, to shut my lights out once and for all. Then, a guy named Robert walked into the bar. His brother Joey used to work for me back in the day, and I hadn't seen Robert for about twenty years. He came up behind me, "Hey, Tony! How are you?" The conversation redirected my thoughts of suicide. I found out that he was driving a car carrier and living in Florida with his brother. He wanted to know what I was up to, so I told him everything. His car carrier was parked outside, and Robert wanted to know if I still had my CDL. "Why don't you jump on the truck with me and leave tomorrow?" he asked. "I'm going to California to drop off cars. Jump on with me, and we'll split the drive."

I told him I couldn't go because my mother died, my father was in hospice, and I needed to get my wife and daughter back in my life. "You're in no shape to help anyone or get your wife back with what you're telling me," he reasoned. So, we partied all night, and I went back to my room while Robert left the next day. That week I ended up back in court three times for various counts against me. Tough week. I went back to the bar, and Robert showed up again. "Robert! I thought you were going to California!" Turns out Robert's trip with the car carrier was canceled. He went to Long Island all week and did runs there, and said he'd be going to California next. I asked if his offer still stood for me to go with him. "Yes, I'll call my boss tomorrow about you. Come on," he said.

I didn't have a cell phone anymore, but I managed to call my father to tell him that I had a chance to drive a truck cross country with a friend. "The first run is to California, Dad. I have to leave New Jersey, but I don't want to leave you, Dad," I struggled telling him.

"Go!" he said. "Your mom's gone. Michole wants to put you away in jail; she don't want you around anymore. I'm your father. Listen to me. Go and don't look back! I'll be all right! You listen to me, Son. Go, go, go! Get on that truck and GO!"

I promised to call him from truck stops along the way.

"Okay, Son. Call me, but leave before you do something stupid!"

"I love you, Dad."

"I love you, Son. Go. I'll be all right. I want you to go."

"Bye, Dad."

"Bye, Son."

That was on October 30, 2003. I got my stuff and left a job that I was going to be fired from anyway.

Our first stop was in south New Jersey at a car auction before driving to San Jose, California. Robert drove in the daytime; I drove at night. We had a bunk in the back for sleeping. We stopped at truck stops to stretch our legs and pick up some Captain Morgan Rum and Dr. Pepper. Robert and I were both fighting all kinds of emotional pain on addiction rollercoasters. Both of us functioned on alcohol plus. I had to use a pay phone to call my dad. We could talk for fifteen minutes before having to drop a quarter! Now and then I'd try to call Michole and talk with Holly, but nothing changed. She wouldn't let me talk to Holly.

In November, just before Thanksgiving, after being on the road for two weeks, we went back to Florida for a week. We wanted to surprise Robert's brother Joey who worked for me as a bouncer twenty years ago back in the 80's. His brother-in-law Billy did all my radiators for cars and some welding when I had my body shop. I remembered going to pick up some work that Billy did for me, but it wasn't ready. I was yelling at Billy. His brother-in-law Joey was outside and heard me yelling. At that time there was a five-gallon bucket of gear lube worth $350 in the back of my truck for a job I was doing. Without me seeing it, Joey took the bucket of gear lube out of the back of my truck. He was a young kid who served up hurt for hurt, and he didn't like the way I yelled at the guy who married his sister!

I didn't discover the missing gear lube until I drove a half hour back to my shop. My mechanic told me it was gone. I threw my .45 under my seat, went back to Billy's welding shop, got out of my truck, and said to Joey (I didn't know him at the time), "Where is my gear lube?!" He said he didn't know, so I pulled my .45 out and stuck it in his face. All of a sudden, he knew where it was. He said he saw a guy take it out of my truck and put it behind some garbage cans over there. I threw it in my truck and left. A couple of years later I ran into Joey at a party at someone's house in New Jersey. I didn't know who he was, but he knew me. He told me that he was the guy on the other end of the barrel of my .45 in his brother-in-law Billy's shop, and that I really freakin' scared him with the gun. We became close friends, and I didn't realize that he bounced for me at the bar. We did a lot of drug dealing and partying together back in the day.

Turns out Joey was doing really well in 2003. He owned a nice house and a nice boat and lived with his wife who was his girlfriend when he worked for me as a bouncer. He had a plumbing company and owned a condo in Deerfield and two triplexes in Pompano Beach. We stayed at his house, and even went out on his boat with him, before buying more liquor and cocaine and going on the road again for all of November and December.

I got back to New Jersey on January 10, 2004 with the intention of taking a car off the back of the truck and driving to Oradell, New Jersey, where my dad was in hospice. I called hospice from a truck stop on Route 17 near the state line. A nurse answered the phone. I told her who I was and that I wanted to let my dad know that I was on my way to see him. "Hold on," she told me while I waited to hear my dad's voice. Instead, I heard the familiar voice of the nurse who was taking care of him. She spoke in a low tone, "Your dad passed away last night."

Chapter 8

What Really Happened

FROM THE TRUCK STOP, I called Michole who said she was sick about what happened to my mom and dad and hung up after telling me, "No, you can't come home or talk to Holly!" I called my cousin Donna who was handling the funeral arrangements for my father. She told me that I needed to get help. She said that she loved me and was worried about me. She told me that the funeral would be in four days, but I told her that I thought the police would be looking for me, and that I probably shouldn't come back. Robert and I headed off to a bar to score some cocaine and drink ourselves into what I called my utopian state, where I felt comfortable and thought I could take on the world. For me, vodka on the rocks and cocaine brought on the ultimate level of high that made me feel like Superman. After the bar closed, we stayed in the apartment of one of the girls we met in the bar. Then, we were ready to hit the road again.

The first stop was to pick up cars in Long Island, and I was going to try to make it back for my dad's funeral, but the cars weren't ready, so we were stuck in Long Island. We found the nearest liquor store so we could watch movies and drink our time away. The next day we got our cars and were on our way to Brownsville, Texas. The cars we picked up were going to a car lot on the U.S. side of the Mexican border. We had to get to Texas in time to unload the cars and load up other cars in Brownsville to bring back to JFK Airport in New York. This would be a tight trip timewise. Robert and I—what a team! We drove to Brownsville in about three days, all the while chasing the high on booze, cocaine, and women. He was fighting his demons, and I was fighting mine. Pure insanity.

Turns out, the owner of the car lot owned the Burger King, a gas station, a bank, and a Mexican grocery store. He lived across the border in Mexico. While we were dropping off the cars, he invited us to an open fire pit barbeque with his friends right there at the car lot! Awesome. Authentic Mexican tacos. And, of course, they had beer, and while they were eating and drinking, the owner of the car lot came up to me with a bottle of Mexican tequila. The boss told me it was the bottle of demons called Tequila Azul. He poured me a shot that slid down my throat like water—no burn, sting, or after taste. He warned me to be careful. He was right. The Azul sneaked up on me. Someone somewhere described a punch from Iron Mike Tyson as a "dorm fridge full of beer falling on you from two stories up," and that's pretty close to what I felt landed on me! I was loop-de-looped and almost back on my feet by ten o'clock when the boss said, "Okay, let's all go out!"

The next thing I knew, we were piled up in the owner's car, driving over the border into Mexico to a Mexican nightclub. A band from America was playing 70's and 80's music, and there were women all over the place. The owner sat us at the bar, threw a gold card on the bar, and said to the bartender, "When their glasses are almost empty, fill them!" Then, he left. So, while we hung at the bar and drank and talked with all the amorous barflies, our glasses were always full. I don't remember sleeping, but I remember breakfast at 7:30. I wasn't feeling well, when I started to drink Captain Morgan Rum. No food. I had to get back to my utopia to get rid of the sickness from the night before. We never left the lot that day. We hung out in the truck all day, drinking and watching movies on the TV in the cab of our truck. We stayed one more day before picking up the cars destined for JFK Airport in Long Island. These were reinforced steel, bomb-proof cars with bullet proof glass—all headed to Iraq. Three Mercedes Benzes and one

Jeep Cherokee were so heavy that we could take only four without being overweight. We left Texas and drove to Robert's brother's house for a visit.

At Robert's brother's house, we took one car off the trailer and threw a plate on it. We left our truck at a truck stop in New Jersey near where his brother lived so we could surprise his brother by arriving in a bomb-proof Mercedes. In moments we were taking it out to a bar and having a good time with it. The Mercedes had two big handles on each side of the car in the front, that, if someone pulled them, the big slide bars inside locked all four doors so no one could open them. We got back to Robert's brother's house safe, stayed the night, and drove to JFK Airport to drop off the cars that had to be shipped to Iraq. My dad had been buried without me, and the disappointment and sorrow of my not being there haunted me.

We drove to New Jersey to pick up cars that belonged to snowbirds—people who flew to Florida for the winter months and had their cars transported. Around the holidays we had no home and no family. I lost everything to my addiction—my family, my home, my job, so we figured, we'd let all the other truck drivers stay with their families, and we'd keep driving. We went to the Fort Lauderdale car auction and picked up cars to take to San Jose, California. After driving about fourteen hours, we got to Breaux Bridge, Louisiana. Robert said we were going to stop for the night, so we pulled into a truck stop, fueled up, and parked. "Come on," he said, and I followed him into a casino with a bar. Robert gave me $100 and told me to go play the slots—Joker Poker, we called it. I ordered vodka on the rocks, started playing a machine, and hit for $1,000! I played a little more until I got distracted by a hot little woman named Cricket who was a truck driver from Louisiana. We partied together until the casino announced its last call just before at 5 a.m. Cricket and every other girl at the bar suddenly got prettier. No need for any anxiety, though. I accepted Cricket's invitation to go with her to her truck for some beer. We walked to her wide load rig, a custom Peterbilt, a beautiful VIT (Very Important Truck) with a kitchen, living room, bedroom, and bath. After a couple hours' sleep, we woke up, and I went back to my truck and woke Robert up before going back to the casino that opened at six o'clock. We got to California in about three days and dropped off the cars in San Jose where we sat for a week before getting another load. It was more time spent partying with Captain Morgan, cocaine, and other truck drivers. It was what truck drivers did at truck stops in 2004. We'd drive and party all over the United States, then have some down time in Florida for a week before going out again for two months at a clip. This was my way of dealing with the pain of so many losses and feeling sorry for and bad about myself. I was drowning in self-pity. I didn't have a clue how lost I really was. There were times when I couldn't stop crying. My mind was a scroll of anxiety and depression. I habitually drank myself into blackouts so I could sleep. Robert was doing the same thing. He had a bad back and walked with a limp. Awful things haunted him. He didn't talk about those things. He drove during the day, and I drove at night in twelve-hour shifts through the deserts of Texas, New Mexico, and Arizona, then into California—890 miles on Route 10 with a gallon of vodka between the seats. Sometimes we stayed in hotels on the weekends or we'd pick up girls in bars and stay with them. On the road I set the cruise control and held the wheel straight, played music, and did some cocaine. That was the normal routine. It's a miracle that we never caused an accident that killed us or someone else.

In 2005, we went to Indianapolis to pick up a load of cars, so I called my friend George from the Greek Islands Restaurant and told him we were going to stop by. He was happy to hear from me. I wasn't feeling too well that day, and George noticed my face. He was concerned that I looked pale, like something wasn't right. He told Robert that he wanted to put me up in a hotel for a night and take me to the hospital in the morning. I told him that I thought I felt a lump on the left side of my stomach. I hadn't noticed it until then, but it seemed to be the size of a small melon. George took a look and wanted to go to the hospital right then, but I told him tomorrow would be fine; all I needed was a good night's sleep in a bed, not sitting up in the driver's seat behind a wheel. That's how Robert and I slept at truck stops—he took the bunk and I slept behind the wheel unless we had a hotel room. In those days plenty of hotels catered to truck drivers by offering them a low rate on a room with two beds and a bath along with a shuttle to a grocery store. A driver had to have a CDL to get these benefits, and sleeping in a bed was a nice break when we were exhausted. That night George left me at the hotel, and I went to sleep. I definitely needed it.

In the morning when George came to get me, I was dizzy. He fast-tracked me to a hospital in Indiana, and, as we walked through the emergency room doors, I passed out. I remember someone asking me if I had health insurance, and when I said I didn't, the person told me not to worry about it.

Hours must've gone by before I realized where I was and what was happening. The doctors performed eighteen hours of emergency surgery because I was bleeding internally from a burst ureter. News to me. If it had been a car part, I might have heard of a ureter, but it wasn't. I'd never heard of it, but later found out that it's a line that connects the kidney to the bladder. My kidneys had stopped working. More news to me: I woke up wearing a urine bag strapped to my side.

Meanwhile Robert got back to Florida without me. Turns out, he fell off the truck and broke his hip, and while he was in the hospital, he found out he had pancreatic cancer. News to him. I was out of work again. But I had a refillable prescription for pain pills which was a good enough reason for me to start washing them down my throat with vodka without a second thought.

Eventually the urine bag was removed, and I reconnected with George, Mike (who was the best man at my marriage to Michole and currently managing a restaurant), Quan (the general manager of another restaurant), and my Greek friend George who was managing his own restaurant in Indy. George let me work at his restaurant, but that didn't last long. Everyone except George's little sister Penny was sick of my chronic inebriation. Penny really wanted to help me, and, most likely, George did too, but he had to do what he had to do. He threw me out of Penny's house and fired me on a night when the temperature had dropped to forty degrees. George knew a guy who ran a homeless shelter in Indy, so he asked a mutual friend to drop me off there. Lucky for me, I had just refilled my prescription for Vicodin®— 280 pills, and I had $200 cash on me. I hung out with the other homeless men, and that's where I laid my head that night after taking a warm shower. I climbed into a bunkbed in a room that held two hundred ninety-nine other men who were dozing off when the lights went out at ten. No women.

At seven o'clock the next morning, I was already washing pills down my throat with vodka. At noon I was hallucinating in a dark place, and you'd think that I'd hit bottom, as they say, but I wasn't even close to that point. A guy came up to me and asked me if I wanted to work, so I got in the car with this stranger and my little bundle of clothes, and we started driving. I asked where we were going. "Columbus, Ohio. We're going to be cleaning a construction site for a company," he answered. We drove for two hours and fifty minutes, talking all the way. His job was to round up workers and get them to job sites.

We arrived. I met husband and wife, Carl and Carol. Carl took me to one of the units where there were about ten other men and women. We started a construction clean-up in one of the apartment buildings—the start of getting five hundred apartments ready to show! About thirty of us workers (both men and women) were hired to thoroughly clean kitchens, bathrooms, bedrooms, and hallways. Carl liked the way I worked, so he made me a supervisor after the second day. We cleaned for fourteen hours a day for two weeks, and when we were finished, Carl asked me to move in with him and his wife to help with the business. It was an opportunity for me to meet the women on the team, and I took full advantage of that because I had my pick, and Carl was all right with that. We went all over Indiana, Ohio, and Michigan cleaning construction sites for well-known restaurant chains. What a booming business! We kept all the equipment in the garage of a nice-sized house in Terre Haute, Indiana, where we were living and partying up a storm day and night. Terre Haute was the methamphetamine capital of the world, which was good because meth took the place of Vicodin® when the prescription ran out. Carl and his son both smoked meth. We worked hard and played hard. Soon Carl started to send me on small jobs without him and his wife. The cycle was insanely vicious. Different hotel rooms with different girls every night. I was a complete lunatic.

One Sunday Carl sent me on a small job for a couple of hours in Indy. I took two guys and three girls with me to clean a small bank. We got back to the house at about two in the afternoon on a day when the Daytona 500 was happening, so, of course, we were going to cook and have a great party. Carl told me that there was a girl named Violet who wanted to meet me and spend time with me, but, because she had been partying all night, she was sleeping. We cooked breaded veal cutlets, string beans, and cauliflower while watching the race with a bunch of people. Then Carl took me aside, showed me a bottle of liquid opium, and told me to try it. I drank only a capful and went straight to the moon without meeting Violet. At about 6 o'clock, when Carl went to find Violet, he came out of the room to let me know that Violet didn't seem to be breathing. I saw her. She was purple, and next to her was that bottle of liquid opium on the night table. I started CPR and told Carl to call the police. Everyone ran out of the house and left me alone with this poor girl, Violet. I called the police myself. The police showed up, went into the room, and called for emergency medical backup. Within minutes, responders came out with Violet on a gurney. They were trying to get her to breathe through an apparatus on her mouth and nose while rushing her to the ambulance.

A detective was on the scene wanting to know who she was, who owned the house, and what was happening. I didn't know anything. Really, I didn't, but I was hauled off to the police station anyway for hours of interrogation. Somehow the police located Carl and brought him to the station for questioning. It was a long night. They let us go in the morning. Carl told me that Violet drank the liquid opium. I don't know where he got it. I didn't ask. Carl was arrested for some old charges and went back to jail. His son and his wife took off and left me at the house, which, I found out, was in foreclosure.

I did what I knew how to do. I called a friend. This time I called Jody, a cook at a restaurant and told him what was happening to me. He picked me up, and we went to his friend's house for a family barbecue. I stayed at his house that night, and Jody took me to work to help him in the kitchen the next day. He was a part owner of the restaurant with some of my other friends, Dino and Chris.

Jody, Dino, and Chris told me I could stay in a fixed-up room by the office in the restaurant, and I could help in the restaurant as a handyman, dish washer, and busboy. I would be their security man after the restaurant closed.

Where did the years go? I was in a deep, dark, lonely place even though I was among people that I knew. I felt alone, lost, and empty. I had no money, and I needed a fix, so I did what I had to do to get some vodka. How convenient! I was being paid to guard all the liquor and all the food after hours in the restaurant and bar! Imagine that. This arrangement lasted for about three months. Then, Chris found a friend of his who was looking for a roommate, so I moved in with him for $75 a week. Jody picked me up for work every day and brought me home at night. Not long after that, the owners became weary of me being blitzed all the time, so I was fired. Again. Not the end of the world. No sir, I got myself a bicycle and found another job and was making $20 an hour at a body shop not far from where I was living in Indy. Eventually I moved out of the $75 a week room because my roommate's girlfriend didn't want me around anymore because I was always drunk. I found a motel room for $150 a week with a liquor store on one side and a restaurant and bar on the other side. The place was surrounded with fast food too. I could get meth in the motel, and there were always plenty of women. I started seeing one.

A friend came up to me and said, "I have a body shop, and I'm looking for some good metal men and painters. You interested?" Of course, I said yes and got the job right after the interview. I started working for $1,500 a week and got paid every two weeks. Wow! Life was good again! So, I moved out of the motel and in with Teresa, the girl that I mentioned a few sentences ago. She had a fifteen-year-old daughter living with her, and I really wanted to try to be a responsible boyfriend, but that wasn't happening. I managed to sleep on the sofa that night after Theresa threw me out of the bedroom, and right after that, I lost my job at the body shop because I was never sober.

My next move was to a metal products company that made hospital equipment for operating rooms in hospitals. I was put on what they called the "deburring" team. My job was to make sure there were no sharp edges (burrs) on the equipment. My team removed the burrs by grinding and sandblasting them. Also, we used tumblers with special stones to deburr pins and brackets that would be used to fuse bones together. I was getting $16 an hour with a lot of overtime by working the night shift. Across the street was a liquor store, and that's where I got my two pints of lunch! I'd sneak them into the bathroom and pour them into water bottles that I could sip on all night. On the way home in the morning, I'd get another quart from the liquor store and drink it until I blacked out in my bed at home. The routine was to sleep all day and get up around 6 p.m. when Theresa got home, then I'd start all over again. I didn't work on weekends, so I would go to a bar, pick up a woman, and go to the back of the hotel next door where I used to stay. Even though Theresa and I broke up, I helped her pay her bills.

I got a call from Joey who was still in Florida. He wanted me to move back to Florida to live with him because I was the only "family" he had. Remember, we were like family back in the day. Joey's brother Robert was the guy who drove trucks all over the country with me.

Well, I was in no position to go to Florida. A few days before he called, when I was walking a girl to a hotel, I slipped on some ice, fell, and broke my ankle. This was the first time I'd ever had pins or plates put in me. I wasn't going anywhere. I was laid up for six months with this ankle! My focus was on getting myself back to health so I could go back to the job I had with the metal products company as part of their deburring team. I got back to that point, all right, but was fired for drinking. I needed money, so I started to sell my tools from working at the autobody shop.

Meanwhile I picked up a job working construction for $15 an hour refreshing Section 8 housing for two rich guys. Hanging out at the bar, I met a new girl named Dawn who happened to be a cross-country truck driver. Becoming an item with her was easy! The time had come for me to leave Indy anyway. Dawn and I left Indy in August of 2006. I drove around with her for about six weeks 'til we got a load to go to Kissimmee, Florida. From there, I called Joey. He drove about three hours from Pompano Beach to get me. I left Dawn thinking she was going to come down to see me from time to time, but that never happened. I moved in with Joey.

Joey wasn't working as a plumber anymore. He had devolved into a prescription drug dealer after figuring out that he could go to different doctors, get prescription pain meds, and sell the meds for big bucks. Powerful meds. Oxycodone. Joey would fake pain in his back at a pain clinic to score a prescription for 180 pills at a clip. Then he'd sell them for $40 a pill. Joey wasn't hurting from pain, lack of women, or lack of money! What a high time it was until Joey got arrested for selling pills.

Suddenly, I realized I was having trouble swallowing anything. How weird. Couldn't even drink right. I wound up in the hospital again. What a rude awakening — my stomach broke through my diaphragm and settled in my chest. My esophagus was twisted like a corkscrew, so doctors pulled my stomach back down and sewed a screen over where my diaphragm had been. For this I was in the hospital for a week. I remembered that years ago, my grandfather was hospitalized for something similar. He became sick and slipped into a coma and was on life support for six months! The doctors said his esophagus had somehow detached from his stomach! That was way back in 1977 before Roseann and I were married. My grandfather recovered from an operation and came home from the hospital on Christmas Eve that year, and the talk was all about how good God was to bring my grandfather home on Christmas Eve! My mother made special meals for him for a long time.

Now, back to Joey. Joey ended up in a mandatory, ninety-day detox program called B.A.R.C. (Broward Addiction Recovery

Center) after he was released from jail. This became a second chance for both of us. Once he was released, we were back in business going to different clinics and different doctors again complaining about pains that we were faking. In two weeks we could get crazy money by selling prescription pain pills for $40 apiece. Joey had to take urine tests after leaving B.A.R.C., so he laid low on taking the pills. He drank instead.

In 2007, I started working on our friend Russell's '67 Oldsmobile Cutlass. Russell was a guitar player, Joey played a bass, and a friend of ours, Louie, had a Drum Workshop drum set (the choice of drummers!) for sale, so we bought it for $500 and started jamming in a tiki bar and soundproof storage unit that Joey built in his backyard. Frankie, another mutual friend who was a mechanic, put up a car tent in Joey's backyard. We towed the Cutlass into the tent for restoration. I pulled the motor, stripped the car down, and started to weld all new sheet metal where it had rusted. What a rust bucket! Russell and his friend Greg had been friends and roommates since high school. Greg had a landscaping business, and when Greg's father died, Greg came into some big money and real estate. Russell had a bad back among other things and wasn't able to work, but Greg treated him like his favorite brother and paid Russell's way. Greg paid me every week to work on Russell's rust bucket of a car! I'd be getting high in the backyard all day while working on this rattle trap. Russell, Joey, and me would take breaks to learn songs and do some jamming in our makeshift studio. Eventually we started to play in bars. There were days when Greg needed help with landscaping, and I fit right in there, too. The odd thing about Greg was, he went to 7:30 Mass every morning at Saint Paul's Church in Lighthouse Point! I'd go with him sometimes, even though I was high, drunk, or both, before going to do the landscaping with him at local residences and businesses. One place was a big car dealership owned by a guy named Tom where we were hired to cut the grass, trim bushes and trees, and clean up around the dumpsters that had tires, bumpers, car doors, etc. in and around them. Some of the trash looked like good stuff, but it was being discarded. We were paid to haul everything away that wasn't bolted down so the dealership wouldn't get written up and fined by Code Enforcement. One time we hauled away an air conditioner that was left on the platform beside the four dumpsters, and, to our surprise, we found out, after we'd hauled it away, that the unit was supposed to go to the owner's new house! Greg had to straighten that one out because we were told to haul away everything that wasn't in one of the four dumpsters, and, for sure, that air conditioner wasn't! I just did what I was told to do.

There was a drink holder on my mower for a Four Loko malt beverage. My drink looked like an energy drink in the cup, but it was 14 percent alcohol and caffeinated, an equivalent of four to six beers, one espresso shot, and one Red Bull. Potent stuff. Greg tried to get me to slow down with my drinking. He didn't realize how sick I was when I didn't drink. I steamrolled myself through days and nights. I had plenty of work with restoring the car and doing landscaping, and I never slowed down with doctor shopping or carrying on with all my antics.

One of the priests, Monsignor Brice, a very godly man in his seventies, took me under his wing. He told me that the church was looking for ushers for Sunday morning Mass. I took the position. Greg transported me in my drunken state after a rowdy Saturday night to the church every Sunday morning for what turned out to be seven days every week counting morning Mass with Greg. My new routine grew within the church to include handyman work for single women from the church. Imagine that.

Despite my efforts to stay on a happy high, I was carrying a dark, lonely place deep inside me from all the messes I'd left behind in New Jersey, Indiana, and other places where I'd overdosed and couldn't remember how I got to where I woke up. Some of these were places where my friends couldn't wake me up at all. They didn't call 911. They left me. Who wanted to be around when police were called for a drug overdose? Nobody! Oxycodone "oxys," alcohol, pot, Xanax bars—I always needed a combo to maintain my utopia. And, there was always something new to add to the combo, something like "spice" or "K2," a synthetic marijuana whose side effects were paranoia, anxiety, panic attacks, hallucinations, addiction, an

increase in heart rate and blood pressure, convulsions, organ damage, and even death. All these wonderful benefits could be bought
at a gas station! How crazy, huh? Even crazier was, I was praying a
lot at Mass every day with Greg, never realizing that I might not be
holding hands with God at all. In my mind, God was on the back
burner. I called out to Him when I was in distress. Other than that,
I didn't know or care where He went or what He was doing.

Suddenly, while I was standing in my friend's living room,
what felt like a bomb went off in my head causing pain like knives
sticking me in the backs of my eyeballs! Apparently, someone
called 911 before leaving me behind. I don't remember being carried out of the house or being slipped into an ambulance. I didn't
hear a siren or anything else, but once again, I woke up in a hospital emergency room surrounded by people who seemed to be trying to save my life! Imagine how many times I didn't care if I woke
up from a blackout or not; still, someone was there to help me
move toward recovery! Looking back, I'm amazed that I survived.
Here was I, the longstanding Champion of Carnality, laid up in an
emergency room again surrounded by doctors who were rushing
around, doing their best to save my miserable life! I blacked out.

When I woke up, I could see machines all around my head,
and I thought my friend Joey was there with doctors and nurses
whose faces were on top of mine saying things that sounded far
away. I didn't miss that whole week of being in a coma. I didn't even
know that an MRI revealed an aneurism in my brain or that doctors
had operated immediately on me the week before. It wasn't long before I realized, too, that I was hooked up to life support and trapped
inside a body that was seizing. If a family member had been found
to pull the plug, that's what would have happened, but it didn't. If
I could have reached the plug, I would have pulled it myself, but I
was paralyzed from the neck down and couldn't even speak!

Learning to walk and talk again took about three months,
actually six months, for me to get back to my new norm of seizures
that threw me into a fetal position on whatever floor I landed.
Whenever that happened, I couldn't talk, and my brain throbbed
like a jackhammer in a wind tunnel. These seizures subsided

somewhat with pills that only made me tired. Doctors and nurses were calling my recovery a miracle. I didn't see it that way. I couldn't wait to get back to my real norm which was indisputable lunacy.

After leaving the hospital, I ditched the seizure meds because they only made me tired, and I loaded up on what drugs and alcohol I could find to reroute myself to blacking out again when I needed sleep. Joey and I weren't seeing eye-to-eye. He didn't want me staying with him anymore, so I left for a while and spent time with my other cronies who were partying all the time in their own ways. Eventually, I went back to Joey's place. We had to stop doctor shopping for pills because by using computers, the authorities discovered what was happening in Florida with "pill mills." Doctors, who had become legalized drug pushers, were being arrested for giving too many pills to people like us. Addictions to prescription pills were at an all-time high in Broward County. Even I got caught in a doctor's office one day. The doctor gave me two choices: walk out of the office or wait where I was for the Broward Sheriff! I left and never went to another doctor for the pills again. I told Joey that I was finished with selling prescription drugs! He didn't like hearing that at all, but he got caught too. That definitely was the end of our prescription drug dealing.

I thought misery was supposed to love company, but living with Joey was uncomfortable to say the least. He'd get drunk and want to fight with me. He blamed me for everything. He had been married and had owned three triplexes, another apartment in Deerfield, and house in Pompano Beach before his wife left him. Joey was in a downward spiral smokin' crack cocaine. He fell behind with paying bills, taxes, etc. and eventually Joey lost all three of his triplexes. The power was shut off at his house, and the house went into foreclosure. We turned water off during the day, but when the water was completely shut off by the city, Joey moved in with someone else. Then, I left and moved in with Larry and his wife. Father Brice brought Larry into my life because Larry needed a job. Greg could use the help, he said, so he hired Larry. The church became important to me. Even though what I was doing was wrong, Father Brice and the church accepted me for what I was—a chronic alcoholic, drug addict.

I was serving at Saint Paul's Catholic Church as an usher at the morning service as well as at the 7:30 a.m. Mass every day with Greg and Larry before work. Monsignor Brice was still fond of me. I would meet him every morning and help him put on his cassock and chasuble. I felt good serving him. I helped him walk to the altar and always made sure he didn't sit on his cape when he sat for the Rosary. The robe had to be draped over the back of the pew. I was always messed up, but I attended to Monsignor Brice with accuracy.

One morning Father Brice was awake, flat on his back on the floor, and it was obvious that his head had just missed hitting the sink when he went down. "Pick me up! I don't want anyone to see me like this," he said. "What's going on with you, Father?" I asked. He didn't answer with an explanation. "Don't tell anyone I fell." So I didn't. I knew that Father Brice had gone through an operation for water on his knee, so I carefully walked him to the altar before every Mass and waited until after the Mass to walk him back down. At that point I didn't know that Father Brice and the parishioners were praying for me. A woman named Gerry told me this much later. Someone with a divine connection *must* have been praying for me all along, though, because I should've been dead chapters ago!

In 2009 I noticed a girl who was walking near me at the church entrance. We were approaching the font of holy water to dip our fingers before leaving Mass. I motioned for her to go ahead of me. That's when I met Gerry, a children's Sunday School teacher, who came to morning Mass. She served at the Sunday services as a lector, commentator, and eucharistic minister. Sometimes she served at the morning Mass during the week. I made it a point to talk to her, and, in retrospect, loved the fleeting moment when I gave her the Kiss of Peace. At my first time ever to do that, I still don't know if she felt more peace than I did because I was drunk. Gerry's girlfriend asked Gerry if I was bothering her. "No, he's okay," she said, before a deacon approached Gerry with, "Tell me if you smell alcohol on him, and we'll take his green jacket and throw him out." Gerry answered, "Why not help him?"

Because Father Brice was becoming frail, the Archdiocese of Miami sent Monsignor Dever, Father Joe, and Father Alonso, all exceptional men of God, to our church. At that time, I was feeling drawn to the church because I respected these men. Even though I had a great relationship with all of them, I couldn't stop smoking crack cocaine with Joey and drinking all day, every day.

One morning in church a guy named Joe offered to me, Greg, and Larry applications to join the Knights of Columbus. Frankie joined too. This was a fun group of men who did all kinds of charities, like the Tootsie Roll Run, which took place at the end of the summer for a month. As Knights, we stationed ourselves at the doorways of supermarkets, churches, etc. collecting money for the mentally handicapped. The donors were given Tootsie Rolls. The Knights also collected money for Respect Life, an anti-abortion organization. We were getting involved with the church. The Knights met once a month and studied to become Catholic disciples. Eventually, I became a fourth degree Knight of Columbus. I started to believe that God was doing something in my life, but, at that time, I was too blind to see it.

Frankie's son went to a Christian academy in the area, and you'll never guess what the mascot was for the football team! A knight! Frankie came up with the idea—he got me a knight's costume, complete with a real sword, and we showed up at the Friday night football game, drunk, but ready to cheer on the football team at the Christian Academy. Every time the team scored, I pulled out my sword, and ran up and down in front of the bleachers hollering, "Go, Knights!" The crowd would go nuts! Families started taking pictures with me, and the school asked me to keep coming to the games at home or away! I became their Mascot, and even made the yearbook! When we became state champs in 2009, the whole team picked me up over their heads and ran all over the field with me while I was swinging my sword and yelling, "Go, KNIGHTS!" At the time, I was curbing my drinking for the games and trying to get my head together because the coaches, the principal, and the parents had befriended me. I could not smell like alcohol in their presence! After the games, though, when Frankie and I got home, we sat on the patio in his backyard beside his pool, and, soon we'd be flying high for all hours of the night. Sometimes friends would stop by to drink beer and party with us. My friends tried to help me by telling me to drink only beer, and, in front of them, I did. Behind their backs, though, I kept up with my crack cocaine, "spice," and vodka.

This insane life style that looked like a drawn-out suicide continued until 2012. My friends loved me and wanted to help me—friends from the church, the Knights, and Frankie, Larry, and Greg. Joey and I were still doing the same thing with drugs and alcohol, and we still weren't getting along for the most part. Joey wanted to blame me for his losses. He was always ready to fight. I wanted to take enough pills to put myself out of my misery—like five Xanax pills washed down with vodka. I wanted to commit suicide, but not really. The feeling was weird. I was lonely. I was locked up in my self-made isolation with a "Keep out!" sign on the door. I was getting sicker and sicker. I was sick when I used and sick when I didn't use. I knew I was dying, but I didn't know what to do or where to turn, and I didn't want anyone else to know.

Chapter 9

The Loneliness of Secrets

LARRY KNEW MY SECRET. Larry, the seminary graduate who was brought into my life by Monsignor Brice a while back, knew everything. He worked doing landscaping with Greg and some of us guys when he needed extra help. Greg, Larry, and I went to morning Mass together. Larry was married, had two sons, and lived in a three-bedroom house in Pompano. He gave me a place to stay.

I kept my gallon of vodka under the box spring and started my routine in Larry's bathroom at about 5 a.m. I didn't take the oxys first because if I did, I'd throw them up. I'd take a swig out of the bottle, then take four or five or more pills. My shakes were so bad that I could hardly get the bottle to my mouth. I had to forcibly hold the vodka and pills down. I was not in good company when I was alone crying, sweating, shivering, and shaking so badly that I couldn't focus. Eventually, I could get up, get dressed, go to church, then to work.

On this particular day, though, I choked at the sight of blood that gushed up from my stomach. I got up off the floor, walked over to the sink, and started to throw cold water on my face. In the mirror, I saw what looked like Death glaring back at me. My face was sunken in—I looked like a skeleton talking to myself, "Tony, what are you doing? Why do you keep on doing this?" I threw more water on my face, and these words came out of my mouth loud and clear, "God, HELP ME!! Please, GOD, HELP ME!!!"

Larry was outside the bathroom door, "Tony, are you okay?"

"What are you doing up?" I wanted to know. He said the Holy Spirit woke him up and told him to check on me.

"I need help, Larry. I can't do this no more. I'm sick when I don't use and sick when I use! I need help! I want to stop!"

"Go back to bed, Tony, and I'll tell Greg you can't work today because you're sick." So, I went back to bed.

In the morning, I got up and did the same thing with the vodka and pills, but when it was time to go to work, we got in the car, and Larry and Greg told me they were taking me somewhere to get help. I was high and felt relief when they told me that. From the back seat I asked where we were going, and they told me it was a place called the Faith Farm Ministries.

"Oh," I said, "for thirty days?"

"No."

"Sixty days?"

"No."

"Ninety days?" I kept guessing.

"No."

"How long?" I wanted to know.

"Nine months," they told me.

"Nine months? Where do I live?"

"There," they said, igniting a memory of a dog that my mother and father got me when I was about eight years old. After a while, they said we had to get rid of him because nobody was home to take care of him anymore so it wasn't fair to the dog. He had no place to run, so they took the dog up to the Catskills in New York State and dropped him off at a farm. That's what happened to Cleo, and I remembered how sad I was then. A year later, my mom bought me a duck. We named him Daffy. Well, Daffy got too big to stay inside the house, so Daffy went to the farm too. A year later we got another dog, and this dog, named Flip, got to be a handful, so we took him to the farm to be free too. Suddenly, the thought hit me, "I'm on my way to the farm, but it wasn't a farm in the Catskills! We were in Florida driving south!"

Chapter 10

Who's on First?

Fort Lauderdale was beaches, bikinis, barbiturates, and booze, wasn't it? Who knew there was a farm in Fort Lauderdale? My friends Greg and Larry knew! And, they were taking me there on October 26, 2012. They had already visited the place and knew Sammie, the soft-spoken intake supervisor who met us at the entrance.

"Is this the guy you told me about?"

Greg and Larry nodded.

"Come on into my office."

Before we could get too comfortable, Sammie asked me, "When did you last use?" "Two days ago," I lied. "Why are you here?" Sammie wanted to know. I told him I was desperate and wanted to change my life. "Do you believe in the Lord Jesus Christ?" he went on. I remember answering "Yes," even though I didn't know anything about Jesus Christ except what my mother told me, which was, "When the chips are down, and things aren't going well, run to your Heavenly Father and pray."

For the first time in a very long time, I felt at ease being with someone who seemed to be there to help me. We talked for a while, then watched a short video about the Faith Farm. When we went to lunch, I couldn't eat. I thought I was hiding my being high and drunk, but Greg, Larry, and Sammie knew. They, and probably everyone else except me, could smell vodka coming through my pores from across the room. Besides that, they knew "the look." Sammie wasn't new to his job, and I wasn't the first person to land on this doorstep after being scraped off the pavement.

Because of my size, I was given the bottom bunk in an open dorm room with seventy-five other guys. We shared nine showers and six sinks. I could've put anything I had in a locker, but I didn't have anything. I tried to sleep in a t-shirt and underwear that was donated by someone somewhere on the outside. Lights went out at 10 p.m., but I couldn't sleep or stay still. My skin itched and crept. Were there bedbugs? I tore my bed apart, but couldn't find whatever was crawling in and out of my body, grabbing my throat, twisting my head, moving around inside me, and wouldn't shut up or stop mocking and poking at me all night long! The lights came on again at 5 a.m. Nothing looked different.

Breakfast was at 6 a.m. Praise and worship in the church started at 7 a.m., and the first class started at 8 a.m. Work started at nine o'clock, and we broke for lunch at 11:30 for one hour before going back to work until 5 p.m. My handyman skills landed me in the Maintenance Department. Specifically, my job was to fix anything on the Farm including donations that went to Faith Farm's thrift store.

On my first day in Maintenance, a guy named Jake came up to me and told me that I didn't look good. No surprise to me. I hadn't slept or eaten since I didn't know when, and, I'd been up all night shaking, shivering, and sweating. I felt like I was flat out on my back stuck to a wide strip of flypaper. Even if I screamed at it, my brain wouldn't stop rattling!

Richard, the supervisor who headed up Maintenance, asked me if I wanted to take the day off and go back to bed. I knew I had to keep moving, so I declined. His second offer was to take me along with him for the day. We would be cleaning a/c filters in all the buildings and residences on the 900-acre property. I climbed into his golf cart and held onto its frame with my white knuckles.

I'd met Jake after lunch in the canteen the day Larry and Greg brought me to the Faith Farm. That day Jake walked up to me, looked down at me, and introduced himself, "I'm Big Jake. You're new around here, aren't you?" Looking up at him turned me into a bobblehead. His size tied my tongue in a square knot. Never before in my adult life had anyone looked down at me to speak. Jake was three times my size! His shoulders seemed wider than the doors behind us! "My name's Jake," he repeated, "and, if you need anything, come and see me." With that, Jake turned and walked away. Greg and Larry advised me to get to know him. Sounded like good advice. Jake was an upperclassman from Tennessee who lived on the third floor. I was on the second floor with all the other newbies.

For much of the first month I couldn't sleep. Couldn't eat, either. Detoxing was a nightmare for me and for everyone else around me. My body was thrashing me for putting it through detox.

Florida's Homeless Act paid for my visits to a doctor three times a week in what they called the "little house." Looking back, I can tell you the little house was kind of like that tent in Joey's backyard back in 2007 where we tore apart that '67 Olds Cutlass rust bucket and got it back up and running. This time, I was the rust bucket. I didn't realize it at the time, but I'd been towed into God's Body Shop. I needed a lot of work, and I knew it. I was about to have my motor pulled, my gears rebuilt, my fuel line replaced, and a lot of rust removed. My loose bearings and wobbly fan belts had to go, too. I needed all new filters. After running my body at full-speed for forty years on vodka and pills, I was facing some serious welding and restoration! Can someone *please tell me*, what on earth does Jesus Christ have to do with rebuilding someone's life!?

At the Faith Farm, six orientation classes were mandatory for six weeks each. We were taught how to read the Bible, how to live life through the Bible, and, in Class Two, what addiction does to a human body. I droned through detox and Class One, then was ready to start Class Two in December, 2012. A few days before Christmas, I woke up, as usual not feeling well. On top of everything else, I was feeling a lot of shame, guilt, and remorse for what I had done to my parents, my wives, my daughter Holly, and my friends. I never made it to my own father's funeral, and I'd lost contact with my Aunt Paula. I wasn't even aware that my beloved godfather, Joey Cass, was gone too. He died in September of 2009 while I was drunk out of my gourd, dressed like a knight, flapping my sword around a Christian high school football field. Me, the Grand Poohbah of Self-indulgence, had been sawing off a large tree branch that I'd been sitting on—just like in the cartoon—sawing myself off from every other friend who ever sat beside me! Suddenly, a human voice broke my stream of self-pity. I heard that the Faith Farm was looking for five more volunteers to be baptized. That sounded good. It snapped me out of my dumps for the time being. I volunteered and was baptized in the Faith Farm church on December 19, 2012.

At noon the day before Christmas, I woke up sober. A lot of the long-timers had gone home for the holiday, and I knew there was no hope for me to get any kind of a pass to leave. I mean, I'd confessed my sins and was baptized, so that should get me into Heaven, if there really *is* one, you'd think! The rest of my life without alcohol and drugs, I mean, would my life just hum along in this place? Give me one bright spot! Even if I *did* have an 8-hour pass to leave for Christmas, where would I go with no home or family?

So, I devised a plan to sneak outside the Faith Farm to the nearest liquor store, which happened to be right across the street, get myself a gallon of vodka, guzzle it down, and wait to jump in front of the next train at the Oakland Park Boulevard crossing. Before I got to the front gate, though, I saw a van filling up with upperclassmen across the way, but that didn't stop me. What stopped me was the voice of a supervisor shouting and motioning for me to get myself over to the van. I hesitated, thinking he'd drop the matter, but he kept yelling and waving his arms until I did what he asked me to do.

"Where are you going?" he wanted to know.

"For a walk," I lied.

"Towards the gate?"

"No," I lied again.

"Is your name on the list?" he asked.

"What list?"

"This list," he answered me, "to go on the bus. . ."

"For what?"

"A Christmas service," he said. "What's your name?"

I told him. I spelled it for him. He looked and didn't find it.

"Hold on," he said. "Spell it again."

I did.

"It's on the list now, Tony. Get on the bus!"

So, I did. I sat on the bus with Jake and postponed my suicide.

"Call to me and I will answer you and tell you great and unsearchable things you do not know."

Chapter 11

Reorganizing Spiritual Bankruptcy

WHEN THE BUS PULLED into a spacious parking area, I asked Jake where we were going. "Calvary Chapel," he told me. "It's a megachurch."

Imagine! This church had 20,000 members! Some of the hundreds of people that I was seeing were dressed up for Christmas and pouring through multiple doors coming into the building! I'd never seen anything like it! And, this was only one of the four services that were planned for that day!

Twenty-five of us guys from the Faith Farm walked through the doors of the megachurch together and were greeted with genuine, welcoming smiles, voices, and nods expressing, "Glad you're here!" "Merry Christmas!" by what seemed like an ocean of nice people. Are they real? Do they mean what they are saying? I broke down and needed something to wipe my tears and my nose—and, hey, this place even gave out tissues! And Bibles!

The 3,800-seat auditorium was near its capacity when we arrived. The lights were out except for some neon and Christmas lights onstage. When the reverb of a thunderous worship band rolled through the crowd, everyone got on their feet and started clapping their hands and worshiping the LORD! Words to the music were on various large screens, and I couldn't keep my arms at my sides, so I raised them, feeling an unmistakable joy that I had never known! I was swept into an overwhelming feeling of total love and acceptance!

When the worship band softened into the background and left the stage, a casual guy came out with a Christmas message. Applause broke out at the sight of him! They loved this dude! My friend Jake nudged me and told me that the pastor had been in recovery at one time. Really? Apparently, he'd had a lot of issues, but when he called out to God, God changed him. That's what I wanted!!!

I didn't know what an altar call was, but at the end of the service, when the pastor invited anyone who wanted to give their life to the LORD to come to the altar, I wanted to run down the aisle, but within minutes, found myself dropped down on all fours like a wounded bear in the middle of the aisle weeping and crawling toward the altar. God was calling my name—me, the Duke of Depravity, the Champion of Carnality—was peeking through the gates of Heaven, and I wanted desperately to go through them —whatever it took—to surrender my life! Strangers lifted my sobbing body off the floor and ushered my rubbery legs to the altar where the pastor prayed over me. There I surrendered my life. All of it. Any speck of good and a whole lot of ugly stuff—I gave all of it to God Almighty! Then, the ushers took whoever went to the altar that day to a room off to the side to explain that we were born again if we confessed our sins, repented, and were willing to go God's way.

The Holy Spirit consumed my pitiful life that day! God lovingly hurled my sins so far away from me that I never knew where or if they ever landed. Never had I experienced such love! It was as if He dropped His big work belt, lifted me up, and, holding me tight, consoled me in His massive arms. My failures were hoisted off my shoulders and laid at the foot of the Cross! I *knew* Jesus was real, that He had spoken on my behalf, that He had paid for my sins, and that I was free to live my life loving Him! I was a changed man, and it was so obvious to my friends. Jake saw it. I had been on Holy ground where God spoke hope directly to me!

> *"He brought me out into a spacious place; he rescued me because he delighted in me." Psalm 18:19 NIV*
> *"I stood there saved—surprised to be loved!" Psalm 18:19b MSG*

Chapter 12

Why Are You Persecuting Me?

AFTER SURRENDERING MY LIFE to Christ at Calvary Chapel on Christmas Eve, 2012, my friends from the Faith Farm stayed up with me most of the night talking about how the birth of Jesus was prophesied and how He was born to save us from evil. I came to understand why Jesus was called our greatest gift, our Savior, and I couldn't wait to go back to that church! I found out that the bus to Calvary Chapel was reserved for upperclassmen only, and I would have to complete Class Four before I could go back! I really *wasn't* supposed to be on that bus on that Christmas Eve, but God put me there with the upperclassmen to keep me and a bottle of vodka off the Oakland Park train tracks!

In January, 2013, I began Class One with an amazing teacher named Stu. The powerful, six-week class was an overview of the Bible that focused on living life through the Bible. In Stu's class I dug into studying the Bible, journaling, and really pressing into using the Bible for my life. Who would have thought this: many of my sins in life matched the sins of some of the people in the Bible! I discovered that I was like the Apostle Paul, who was also called Saul of Tarsus in his sinful nature. Saul was an egotistical maniac, a manipulator, just like I was, except I wasn't actively searching out Christians and killing them like Saul was. As a Hebrew Pharisee, Saul hated Christians and thought he was doing God a favor by killing them! God struck Saul down on the road to Damascus, and spoke to him in an unmistakable voice,

"Saul, Saul, why are you persecuting me?" (Acts 9:4)

"Who are you, Lord?" Saul must have spluttered.

"I am Jesus, whom you are persecuting. Now, get up and go into the city, and you will be told what you must do."

The brilliance of God's light blinded Saul for three days. In his blindness, Saul saw who God really was! God even directed the hurting, repentant Saul to a place in Damascus where Saul regained his sight and strength. Saul's eyes were open to a living God who had great purpose for his life, and Saul began using his Roman name Paul as he traveled and became known as a committed follower of Christ, an uncompromising defender of Christians, and, perhaps one of the greatest Christians the world has ever known! His writings, inspired by God, take up much of the New Testament.

Class One woke me up to that and other great stories recorded in the Bible! All along, I thought the Bible was full of stories of God punishing people who weren't following His strict rules, but the Bible clearly shows, time after time, how God rescues and restores some of the stubbornest people the world has ever known! Class One woke me up to the fact that God's laws were made to protect us and show us the best way.

Class Two was about addiction. We learned facts that showed how the addicted brain operates, how addiction can destroy the body, and, eventually crush a person's life, family, business, finances, etc. Lots of facts! Alcoholics can live to be about fifty-five years old, I found out, and there I was at the Faith Farm at age fifty-five after being an alcoholic since I was fifteen! That had to be a "God thing!" When we were given a worksheet with all parts of the human body on it and were asked to highlight each part that could be harmed by alcohol, I had *all* the parts highlighted! That was another eye opener!

Class Three was on setting boundaries, Godly goals, and priorities, something I had never even considered. Setting boundaries is accepting a balance of choices in life so that I won't go back to my old selfish ways. We learned that it's okay to say this one-word sentence: No. We learned to say NO to drugs, drinking, adultery, and NO to going back to the way we came into the Faith Farm! Setting boundaries meant being ready for changes and seasons of God's will for my life while staying humble through it all. Humility is a big part of learning boundaries—setting boundaries without pride and ego while moving forward in life the way Jesus lived. I often ask myself, "What would Jesus do?" in setting up boundaries that are pleasing to the will of God. Without boundaries, I could become co-dependent. Learning about boundaries helped me recover in a big way. I learned to set up real obligations to myself, and how to be "selfless," not "selfish." All of this was new to me, but setting priorities, such as church, work, home, family, and ministry became another way for me to stay focused on succeeding. As I progressed through these classes at the Faith Farm, I knew that God was changing me. I learned that I couldn't hide anything from Him! More than that, though, I didn't *want* to hide anything from the One who loved me enough to save me, even from myself, and light a path for me out of my dreadful darkness!

> *"For all have sinned and fall short of the glory of God, and all are justified freely by His grace through the redemption that came by Christ Jesus." Romans 3:23–24*

Chapter 13

A Familiar Face

MARCH 3, 2013. MY birthday. I celebrated my fifty-sixth birthday sober at the Faith Farm, and that was BIG for me! A huge accomplishment! Also, I moved into Class Four, and that meant I would be going back to the church where I gave my life to Jesus on Christmas Eve, 2012. I found a nice black suit in our thrift store, and I was very happy boarding the bus with about twenty-five other upperclassmen that Saturday night! Jake was there, too.

We found seats up front in the middle section, and before the service, I took time to go to the men's room. On the way, I stopped in my tracks as I caught a glimpse of a familiar face. Could that be Gerry, the girl I met and served with at the nine o'clock Mass in the Catholic church in Pompano? The girl I gave the Kiss of Peace? I hadn't seen her in six months! And, the last time I saw her I was a nutcase! She looked like an angel that dropped in front of me out of the ceiling of the church! She was as beautiful as ever! It *was* Gerry! I fumbled my greeting, "Hi, Gerry!"

"Hi, Tony! You look great," she answered. "I thought you were at the Faith Farm."

I cleared it up for her, "We come here on Saturdays as a part of the program."

Gerry was sponsoring a girl in recovery who wanted to celebrate her first year of sobriety by visiting Calvary Chapel to listen to the popular pastor. The girl had no church at all, and Gerry was still going to Saint Paul's on Sundays. Gerry told me that she had prayed for me for five years to get help, and that God answered her prayer when Larry and Greg told her that they took me to Faith Farm. She saved a seat for me to sit with her group after I came back from the men's room. We walked out of the service together that night and had a few brief moments to talk all about the curriculum that I was learning. I told her that I hoped to see her again the following week. "Sure," she said. "Same time. Same place." All the guys on the bus wanted to know "Who was *that*?"

Class Four was being taught by the man who let me get on the bus with the upperclassmen the first time I went to Calvary Chapel. He also supervised donations, trucks, pick-up donations of furniture for the Farm to sell—all parts of subsidizing the Farm for the future life of the program at the Faith Farm. Class Four was an amazing class that taught us principles from the book, *The Purpose Driven Life*, by Rick Warren. In this class we learned to view ourselves through the eyes of Jesus, and the big question seemed to be, "What on earth am I here for?" This helped me develop a relationship with Jesus Christ, and, how that, I've come to know, changes everything! We were taught that we were planned for God's pleasure and to become a part of His family. We were created to become like Christ and shaped for serving God, which is our "calling" or "mission." The workbook that we studied for forty days was so powerful; it woke me up to realizing that I am worthy because my identity is found in Christ! Imagine that! Not only is He rebuilding me after a good frame-off restoration, like me and the guys used to do with junk cars, but He gave me a new title that claimed me as His own! I became a Child of God!

Chapter 14

That's What I Want!

THE FAITH FARM'S FURNITURE Department sold all kinds of curios and, of course, donated furniture. A very likable guy named JoJo, a former baseball player, high school teacher, and dedicated coach for years, was one of my classmates who was in charge. I was with him when a customer named Derrick came into the store and asked us to go with him to Celebrate Recovery at Calvary Chapel on Friday night. This is the first time we were hearing about Celebrate Recovery. Richard, our director, said he had heard about it and asked us to check it out.

What an amazing night! About 175 people there were struggling like I was with sobriety, fear, and anxiety, and their conversations were my story, as well! The two leaders, Cleve and Skip, each had fifty years of sobriety! God was telling me that this is where I belonged. After having a bite to eat and some fellowship, everyone went into a general meeting that began with passionate worship music. The words were on the screens, and everyone sang together. Then there was a testimony or a teaching on the Twelve-Steps to recovery based on Bible scriptures. All of it made sense. Following that, we chose which small group we wanted to attend based on topics such as, drug and alcohol addiction, sexual integrity, anger, and co-dependency. The Director of the Faith Farm was happy to hear the good report and decided to allow the upperclassmen to come along with us. So, every week about sixteen of us went to Celebrate Recovery. I volunteered to be a male greeter at the front table with a girl named Carmen who greeted the women. We greeted the guests and gave them name tags. This was a very nice way for me to meet people in Celebrate Recovery. God had opened another door for me.

In the meantime, a new man named Pastor Douglas Lidwell came to the Faith Farm. He and his wife, two sons, and a daughter named Dallas would eventually move to Florida from his hometown in Illinois where he used his deep, clear voice as a radio announcer. He preached a sermon about the importance of marriage that brought the whole church (about 180 people) to the altar! Anyone who hadn't already given his life to Christ did so that night! The Pastor and his wife and family went back to Illinois, and the guys at Faith Farm went to the Director the next morning at worship and expressed their desire to get Pastor Douglas back. That morning, one more pastor was supposed to come from Chicago to preach, and we were advised to hear him before making a snap decision. The consensus of the men at Faith Farm was that the pastor from Chicago didn't hold a candle to the sincerity, compassion, and knowledge of Pastor Lidwell. Everyone wanted the Faith Farm to hire Pastor Lidwell, and that happened.

I was on my way to starting Class Five, which was a powerful series of studies such as, *The Man I Want to Be*, *The Pursuit of Holiness*, *The Alpha Series*, and *Anger Management*. I would also be required to write a personal testimony for graduation. Before I could graduate, I would have to complete six weeks each of Class Five and Class Six.

In the church one time I had a vision of a tall cross on the altar. I could see the dimensions and details in my mind: three angle channels put together for the vertical and horizontal. I pictured a beautiful steel cross painted white to represent my vision of purity in Christ to fight addictions. When I took the replica to the Board at the church, the Board advised me to wait for the new pastor to come because the decision would be his. March and April went by.

I finished Class Five with an A plus, a grade that I'd never achieved in school!

I felt God brought Pastor Lidwell and his family to the Farm. God spoke through him, and I sensed a strong bond with him. After Pastor Lidwell moved in, I told him about the cross that I built because I believed the altar at the Faith Farm needed it. We were in tune! Pastor Lidwell told me that he was praying for a cross for the altar, and I was excited to show him the demo that I made.

When Pastor Lidwell saw what I made, he looked like he saw a ghost! He stared at it without saying a word. Didn't he like it? I *had* to ask him what he thought!

"Where did you get the design?" he wanted to know.

"It was a vision from God. . ."

"No, where did you get that design?" he went on.

"From God," I insisted.

"Hold on a minute," he said pulling his phone out of his pocket.

He showed me a picture of himself and asked me if I'd ever seen the picture. I hadn't. He told me to look closer at his shirt. His shirt was black with a small cross on each collar tip, and the Crosses matched my demo exactly! In disbelief, he asked me again if I had ever seen the photo, and, not lying, I said, "No."

"That's the Cross I want on the altar! Can you size it up for our pulpit?"

He asked me to draw up the plans in diamond plate silver and show him. I drew up the plans that night and had the go-ahead from Pastor Lidwell to build it! I prayed for the materials that I needed and felt God's presence walking through the Maintenance Department showing me exactly what I needed to build the frame. Jesus spoke clearly as we walked through what was at hand. In almost no time, I was able to weld the frame, grind it, and paint it. Joe, my supervisor, got me the chrome diamond angle plate. Then, I mounted the Cross to the pulpit frame and put spotlights behind it sideways so that when the church lights dimmed, the Cross glowed onstage as if it were floating. Pastor Lidwell thought it would be a nice idea to unveil the Cross at the

Wednesday night service and tell how the design came into being, so that was the plan.

Just thinking about my first time speaking in front of the group that Wednesday night gave me antsy nerves. Too, I knew that Gerry was coming to hear me talk about the new Cross! The pulpit was covered when everyone came into the church that night. I was so jittery that Pastor Lidwell told me to look at the clock on the back wall when I spoke so I would look like I'm speaking to the crowd. Sounded like a good idea, if I could only remember to do it! I prayed and squirmed for a good half hour through the praise and worship and the tithes and offerings before Pastor Douglas introduced me. Then, I got up and told the story of how Pastor Lidwell's vision matched the one God gave me to build the Cross for the altar. Finally, it was unveiled! Gerry gave us some holy water that she got when she visited the Jordan River in the Holy Land, so we blessed the Cross with the holy water, and Pastor Lidwell spoke and read Scriptures before ending the service with an emotional altar call that drew guys from their seats.

Earlier that day, while we were setting up the Cross, a friend of the founder of Faith Farm gave me a book that he, the founder, known as "Pappy," used in his Bible teaching. The friend simply handed it to me, told me that Pappy would want me to have it, and walked away. I never met Pappy, but I knew Pappy's daughter Dolores who told me all about her father and how he built the Faith Farm. After the altar call, I felt that Pappy was smiling from Heaven, so I left Pappy's book at the altar and went back to my room with the sweet thought that God had put every detail of this whole event together! I like to think that my friend Pastor Douglas Lidwell and I met at the foot of the Cross!

Pastor Lidwell, the Cross, and me

After the unveiling, the Cross remained on the altar. Pastor Lidwell and I both spoke from behind it. God started to mold me into a speaker by sharing my testimony, Bible verses, and the Good News of the Gospel. Encouraging my classmates from the pulpit on Wednesday evenings was a blessing! Gerry was coming to hear me speak on Wednesdays, too, and just seeing her there meant a great deal to me.

I was still attending Celebrate Recovery at Calvary Chapel on Friday nights. Gerry was able to drive me to the meetings before going to her girls' Alcoholics Anonymous meetings, and then she'd pick me up afterward. Sometimes she stayed with me at Celebrate Recovery.

My graduation from the Faith Farm was scheduled for July 21, 2013. That weekend Gerry had previous plans to go to Cape Cod for her family reunion, and she was very disappointed to know that she would miss my graduation. The graduation would be recorded, so I told her not to worry because she could watch the video with me when she came back. But on a Sunday, the week before I was going to graduate, Gerry showed up at the Faith Farm in the late afternoon. Security came to my dorm where I was doing homework and told me that Gerry was there to see me. I saw her getting out of her car and getting a shopping bag out of the trunk when I walked outside the dorm. She seemed unusually nervous, telling me that she needed to talk with me *now*, but where could we go on the Faith Farm's ten-acre lot with 250 people? Out in the field there were two chairs under a tree that I believed God put there for us, so that's where we went. Gerry opened the shopping bag and gave me a beautiful, leatherbound devotional called *Jesus Calling*, by Sara Young. Engraved on the outside was "Big Tony." Gerry handed it to me and said, "Well done, good and faithful servant!" She also gave me some Christian t-shirts for my graduation. Then, she asked me to turn my chair to face her and hold her hands.

"Look me in the eyes," she said.

I was nervous. So was she. I looked into her eyes and took her hands, all the time wondering what exactly was going on. She continued,

"You are my hero!"

"Oh, because I'm graduating next week?" I answered with probably the dumbest look.

"No," she answered me before repeating, "You are my hero!"

There was a long pause that she broke by saying, "I've fallen in love with you, Tony, and I'm scared. I haven't dated a man for forty years."

I was shaking and nearly fell off my chair. "I have feelings for you too, Gerry, but I have nothing! I'm in a homeless recovery program and have lost everything."

She looked at me and said, "You've got me and you have God with you too. That's all you need!"

Not knowing what God had in store for me, us, or our future, I told Gerry that we should take it easy and date for a while. When we kissed, I was scared and freaking out that this beautiful angel of God had fallen in love with me, and I had fallen in love with her, like in a fairytale. Gerry was out of my league, I thought. How was I going to do this the right way after what I had done to two other wives and my daughter? I was a brand-new Pentecostal Christian for about nine months. Wow! In nine months a new baby is born! On July 21, 2013 that new life was me!

The blessing in Faith Farm Ministries was how God was flexing His muscles, showing me how powerful He was in helping me climb mountains. On the day I graduated, each graduate got money that had been put aside at the Farm for the nine months of work done. It amounted to $150. (seven dollars a week), and I was paid the week before graduation. I used the money to rent a pure white tux, a red vest, red bow tie, and red handkerchief. To me, the white tux symbolized being born again. This time, in Christ!

Stu took me aside on my day of graduation and said, "You are going to be last, and I want you to let the Holy Spirit speak. All the other guys were given fifteen minutes. You have as much time as you want. Do the testimony that you wrote. One other question: If I let you go home, what are the chances you will drink?"

I guessed, "75 percent"

"Good!" he said. "You will not be leaving yet. You are going to stay for a while longer."

"What do you mean, Stu?" He answered me by telling me not to think about it anymore and just to get through that day.

All my friends were at the amazing graduation! I even got to play the drums with the worship band! Eight out of forty guys made it through graduation! After each graduate gave his testimony, it was my turn to speak. I don't remember exactly what I said during those twenty-five minutes, but I know this: the Holy Spirit spoke through me loud and clear! Afterward, all my friends, including Greg, Larry, Frankie, and Lenny, went out to dinner with me, and I was feeling that I had been a part of a beautiful day that reflected much accomplishment.

Graduation Day 7/21/2013
Richard Rosendo (left), Stu Lane (right)

The day after graduation was a Monday. My friend Oliver offered to take me back to the tux store to return my rentals. For a
while I had been riding a three-wheeled bicycle with a tool box
built on the back. All my tools were in the box—a Makita screw
gun, a drill, batteries, and a battery charger, plus all kinds of hand
tools for the many projects on the Farm. I was on call for any kind
of problem requiring maintenance—water leaks, clogged toilets,
electrical problems, etc. All the staff lived on the property in the
Faith Farm's twelve houses. Plus, there was a dorm with three

floors that held two hundred guys, and four donated hotels that were turned into apartments, plus the mechanic's garage and the appliance center. All of this kept me busy! Before I went with my friend to return my rented tux, I parked my three-wheeled bicycle by the front of the main office.

On our way to the tux store, an electrical maintenance partner called to tell me that someone stole my bicycle with all my tools! I laughed because I was sure he was joking. How could that happen with everyone around in broad daylight? But, when we got back and went to the office, my bicycle wasn't there. I went outside and looked everywhere thinking the guys hid it from me, but my friend Brian found me and told me no one was lying or joking; someone *did* steal the bike with all the tools! He repeated it emphatically. Just then a supervisor named Larry drove up and said, "I tried to stop them but they were fast!" We went into the furniture store and looked at the security camera, and on camera there he was, riding off with my bike and tools! Larry and I got in his truck and went out into the community where we saw a guy riding my three-wheeler! When I jumped out of the truck and grabbed him, he told me he'd just bought it! All the tools were gone! I tried to hold onto the guy, but he broke loose and was gone by the time the cops came. I got the three-wheeler back, and the Faith Farm bought me all new tools.

About a week later, when I was riding my three-wheeler going out to change a/c filters in the office, Stu Lane pulled up beside me on his golf cart and said we needed to talk. He asked me to meet him in the maintenance shop. When I got into Stu's golf cart, he looked me in the face and said, "I've waited twenty-five years for you to show up!"

"Stu, what are you talking about?"

"The whole program," he said. "I watched you and met with you once a month. I watched God anoint you. I also talked to all your teachers, and they said you are anointed to teach, Tony! I've waited twenty-five years to turn over my Class One to someone whom I felt was anointed to teach, and that person is you! God chose you! So, we are going to put you in an apartment on the

Farm, so pick your furniture out, and you'll get a computer. I'll give you all the teaching for Class One. Study the lessons. Add what you want to add and what you feel the Holy Spirit wants you to add. Also, you are going to be in Student Leadership Services. We'll pay you one hundred dollars a week, and you'll stay as a Maintenance Supervisor for a while before being moved to Supervisor of the Furniture Department, so I can work closer with you. And, oh, by the way, you'll have to stop smoking."

I'd wanted to quit the disgusting habit of smoking for a long time, but couldn't. Thinking about a cigarette made me want to light one up. How disgusting is that? The only way I knew to stop smoking was to ask God sincerely to show me how break the habit! I'd been told that a person won't go to Hell for smoking, but, for sure, he'll smell like he's already been there!

Soon I noticed that if I lit a cigarette and tried to inhale it, I would gag and cough—like I probably did when I smoked my first cigarette way back when. Then the cigs started having a bad taste. Still, I kept resisting the cold turkey stop. Why? Now I know why!

One afternoon at work I lit up a cigarette, took a deep puff, and got an intense pain near my heart that bent me over and made me sweat. Whoa! Felt like the Big One! I threw the cigarette aside, sat down, and sent up another foxhole bargaining prayer, "God, please heal me from whatever that was, and I won't smoke again. I'll never pick up another cigarette!"

That day I went to Pastor Douglas' office and asked him to please give me fifteen minutes to speak before the service that evening, and he said okay. I walked up to the pulpit in my work clothes and piled everything that was in my pockets—my personal phone, my Faith Farm phone, my walkie-talkie, all my keys (maybe a hundred?) to the Farm, my wallet, pens, and a money clip with a few bills in it—onto the pulpit and pointed out how much "stuff" I'd been carrying all day. Then I pulled out a pack of cigarettes and said, "What do I need these for? They are killing me!" I told my friends how I prayed and asked God to take them away from me and how I felt once again that Death was after me like when I was using drugs and throwing up blood.

With that, I walked in front of the Cross at the pulpit, crushed a new pack of cigarettes, and left them at the foot of the Cross. Amazingly, about twenty guys came up to the pulpit, left their cigarettes at the Cross, and we stood arm-in-arm as the Pastor prayed over us for healing! Again, my Savior showed up and saved me from the clutches of Satan! There is such great freedom that comes from never having to live with cigarettes again! Seems to me, quitting smoking is as difficult, if not more difficult, than quitting drugs and alcohol.

Breathing God-given air feels so good! My health feels good! My heart and soul feel good! I feel I've been made new and alive!

> "Therefore, if anyone is in Christ, the new creation has come:
> The old has gone, the new is here!" 2 Corinthians 5:17 NIV

I have learned that my body is the temple of the Holy Spirit. *That's* what I want living inside of me!

Soon after that I was given the Class One curriculum to teach in six-week intervals. I studied them with Gerry on Saturdays and Sundays before teaching *Overview of the Christian Life and How to Live Life Through the Bible*. On the first Monday that I began teaching, I was shaking in my boots. I sat behind the pulpit that I built and looked at forty guys looking back at me for help. Prior to this, the guys were only here for six weeks of orientation, so they were brand new to me. The first thing I did was to tell everyone, "Let's pray." I put my head down and started to pray for the Holy Spirit to come into me and fill me up with a fresh outpouring. I turned my will over to Him completely. I don't remember what I taught in the first class, but I *do* remember the Holy Spirit was answering all the questions! It was such a God-filled teaching! This was a great encouragement to me to live for loving teaching! After the first six weeks, I was called into the office to review the student survey of my teaching. The CEO, Director, Assistant Director, and Stu Lane told me that whatever I was doing, I should keep on doing it because the students had nothing bad to say about my first six weeks of teaching. All of them respected what I stood for—My Father's Business and Agape Love. Stu believed that God had ordained me to teach!

We then watched the movie *Hacksaw Ridge* where a conscientious objector saved seventy-five guys' lives behind enemy lines. Every time he went behind enemy lines to bring another guy out, he would say, "God, one more! Just one more!" That's how I felt while teaching at the Faith Farm!

Not long after that, Stu introduced me to Pastor John C. Glenn from the Freedom Ranch in Okeechobee, Florida. Pastor Glenn authored the *Alpha Series*, which teaches practical ways to apply the Gospel to our daily lives. In six weeks, Pastor Glenn taught me how to teach the *Alpha Series*, and in due time, I was teaching Classes One, Four, and Five.

At 4 a.m. I woke up and got ready to spend the first ninety minutes in the church, doing a quiet time with God and getting ready to teach. Breakfast was at 6 a.m. and praise and worship at 7 a.m. followed by my classes from 8 a.m. to 2 p.m. with a one-hour lunch break. From three o'clock until 6 p.m. I was in the Furniture Department. Dinner was at six. Then, from 7 p.m. until eight, I ran extra duty with the guys who got yellow slips for misbehaving. Doing God's work was so awesome! I had two offices in the church, one for Maintenance and the other for my classes. I was put on the Faith Farm's insurance policy so I could drive the upperclassmen to Celebrate Recovery at Calvary Chapel where I was serving as a male greeter. I felt Heaven on earth every day! Such immense blessings were being poured into my life! God was molding me His way for service in His Kingdom.

Gerry and I were dating on Wednesday nights. On Sundays, I ushered for the morning Mass at 7:30 at Saint Paul's Catholic Church where Gerry and I met, then went back to the Faith Farm for the 10 a.m. service where I was the head usher and Pastor Douglas Lidwell's righthand man. Often, I was asked to do a Sunday or Wednesday night service. Imagine! After I'd been living on drugs and alcohol for forty years with a stone-cold heart toward people, especially women, God began shaping me into being the man He created me to be! I was living the Bible and building my new foundation on the Rock of Jesus!

Yes, *that's* what I want!

"The LORD your God has blessed you in all the work of your hands. He has watched over your journey through this vast wilderness. These forty years the LORD your God has been with you, and you have not lacked anything."
Deuteronomy 2:7 NIV

Chapter 15

Jesus Knows Me—This I Love

In August of 2013 I woke up to a gut-wrenching realization that a lot of the guys were dying after leaving the Faith Farm. They had bought the lie that after being clean and sober, they could handle the same amounts of drugs and alcohol that they took before detoxing. The truth is, their bodies couldn't tolerate their previous lives of addiction, so they were overdosing much too often! It was then that God gave me a vision to write a sermon on the drug and alcohol high versus the Holy Spirit high and "Don't leave before the miracle happens!" With the drug and alcohol high, an abuser needs a drug dealer or a liquor store to purchase his poison and always has to be chasing that good utopian high. When an addict is trying to kill pain, he is always listening to the lies of Satan. An addict getting high is committing a slow suicide because he or she doesn't want to live like that anymore. Insanity is a vicious cycle! But when a person gains a personal relationship with Jesus, he drops to his knees and starts praying to Jesus and meditating on Him. That's when the Holy Spirit begins His transforming presence. It's free. You don't have to lie, steal, or cheat to get it. You will thank God that you're free at last! Caution: Don't leave the program before the miracle happens! What is the miracle? The miracle is when God takes away from you all temptations for drugs, alcohol, lying, stealing, lust, smoking, swearing, people pleasing, and manipulating.

That is the miracle. That is a part of the sermon I wrote for the August 15th Wednesday night service.

So, I talked with the Pastor, and he told me to do it. The night before, on August 14th, I was sleeping in my apartment when I started to dream about the sermon for the next night. But this dream had a twist because while I was dreaming, I heard a voice loud and clear coming from a presence over my bed. I saw a big figure standing on the side of my bed who said in a deep voice, "Tony, while you are on the altar doing the Holy Spirit sermon, I want you to bring Gerry up to the altar and ask her to marry you." I sat up fast and heard the voice coming from a bright light in my room repeating the request to bring Gerry up to the altar and propose to her! I shook my head and sat on the edge of my bed listening to the voice repeating, "Bring Gerry to the altar and ask her to marry you!" I got up and walked around the room. I checked the doors. All of them were locked, and I was the only one there. I sat up all night from 2 a.m. During that time, I opened my Bible, and the page that was facing me was the story of the first miracle of Jesus, the wedding in Caanan when Jesus turned the water into wine!

At 5 a.m., I went to the church, and then went to breakfast at six. Worship started at seven, and I was still mentally engaged with what I'd experienced in my room with the voice and the light and what the voice told me to do. Without telling anyone, I taught my class at 8 a.m., and after the class, I ran to the Pastor's office and told him that I *had* to talk to him! He told me to come in and pull the shade on his door so no one would interrupt us. He sensed the urgency in my appearance and voice and asked if I was all right. I wasn't sure, but I started to tell him what happened the night before.

He looked at me and said, "Wow. That sounds like our Holy God sent you an angel and gave you a command!" I was bewildered. I looked at him when he asked me what I was going to do about it. I told him I needed a ring! He told me to look in the jewelry case at the thrift store on the property. Within minutes I was there, holding an engagement ring that I was certain was too small, but the voice in my head assured me it was the right one. The worker at the jewelry case told me to take the ring and worry about the money for it later. He let me know that he would be at the service that evening.

At noon I called Gerry and was prompted by the Holy Spirit to tell her that I was deeply in love with her. She answered me, "I'm sure one day you will show me how much you love me." From there I went back to Pastor Douglas' office and told him about the ring and the phone call. He saw all of it as a confirmation. My insides were freaking out.

Gerry brought a dinner basket with sandwiches so we could sit at a picnic table before the service that night. My head kept echoing that the ring I bought would be too small, but, as we were eating, I noticed her tiny fingers, and was amazed and relieved that the ring might be exactly the right size. God knew! Then, I became obsessed with wondering how I was going to get Gerry up to the altar! The Pastor told me to simply start the service, and let God work everything else out.

The service started. We sat in the front row and worshiped with the band. The Pastor gave the announcements, took the offering, and introduced me as the speaker for the evening. I got up and started my sermon. Near the end, the Holy Spirit prompted me to talk about Gerry and me, how we had met, how she had prayed for me, and how she had been sponsoring fifteen women at the Bottom Line Alcoholics Anonymous Group. I also talked about how I had been working on the Faith Farm with 185 guys, and how God brought us back together at Calvary Chapel. The words rolled off my lips, "Gerry, come up on the altar beside me!" She walked up to where I was, and as she stood beside me, I looked into her eyes and said, "Gerry, by the grace of God and by the power of the Holy Spirit, will you marry me?" She looked into my eyes, smiled, and said, "Yes!" I placed the engagement ring on her finger. Perfect fit! I turned to the congregation and said, "That's the power of the Holy Spirit!" The applause and joy resounded throughout the congregation! When the church calmed down, Gerry and I took our seats, the Pastor took the pulpit and said, "I forgot what I was going to do!" He composed himself and started talking about a man who was fighting addiction for forty years before he came to the Faith Farm—a man who went through the program for nine months. A man who graduated. A man who was blessed by God with a beautiful angel. And, a man who asked her to marry him, and she said, "Yes!"

What a God-filled night! After the service, people ran up to congratulate us, hug us, and cheer us on! But it wasn't all about us! It was about our loving and powerful God and how His mission is to rescue and restore those who trust Him! It was about how He transformed two alcoholics and lived through them to give hope to others! What a miraculous revelation! God spoke to me, God spoke to Gerry, and we listened and obeyed our Heavenly Father!

When we said yes to God!

"For the message of the Cross is foolishness to those who are perishing, but to us who are being saved, it is the power of God." 1 Corinthians 1:18 NIV
"Today, if you hear His voice, do not harden your heart . . ." Hebrews 3:15 AMP

Chapter 16

That's My Tat & Meet the Family

I WAS STILL LIVING at the Faith Farm in 2013 when Gerry started to talk about spending our Christmas together with her family in Colorado. She wanted me to meet her son and daughter-in-law and their two boys who would become my new family once we were married. Gerry wanted to spend a week in the Colorado Rockies with them at their ski house. Then, from there, we could fly to Utah to be with her daughter and her five girls, Gerry's granddaughters! Gerry's first husband, the father of her son and daughter, had died of colon cancer.

On my arm was a tattoo of Michole and my little girl Holly, so, I'm thinking that when I go to Colorado and Utah with these tattoos, what can I say? Awkward! I had time; this was only September. Pray, pray, pray in the meantime about this!

Pastor Douglas and I were having lunch and talking about everything in general one day in the cafeteria, when I brought up my tattoos and how I felt I needed to do something about them before I could marry Gerry and meet her family. My thought was to see a tattoo artist and ask him to make a tribal band around my arm that would cover Michole's image, but leave Holly's face. Pastor Doug locked eyes with me and said, "Why don't you ask the tattoo guy to put the face of Jesus there with your daughter?" I was stunned. Why hadn't I thought of that!? What a great idea! Not two minutes later, my friend Derrick walked up to our table and said to us, "Look at this picture I drew of Jesus! I'm going to get it tattooed on my arm!" My jaw dropped. The Pastor looked at me and Derrick and said, "Do you have a wireless communication to God?" I looked at Derrick and asked if I could see his drawing. He handed it to me. "Do you want it?" he asked. I looked at it and knew it was the one God was giving me, so when I told Derrick that I'd like to have it, he handed it to me.

A week later I took the drawing of Jesus to a tattoo artist who had a shop nearby and told him that I wanted him to make changes on my forearm to show Jesus with my daughter Holly. After two, four-hour sessions and with a Faith Farm discount, the tattoo, even though still damp, was better than I had imagined! The eyes of Jesus to this day seem to look past me to my Heavenly Father, and my daughter Holly is safe right there with Jesus! This tattoo has become a powerful witnessing tool for me. Most people, especially the next generation, ask me about it when they see it, and that opens the door for me to share the Gospel. I say it over and over that God is so amazing! I believe wholeheartedly that He continues to make me into the man He created me to be with a second chance at a new life!

In October, Gerry told me that her daughter was coming from Utah for a long weekend so I could meet her before our trip to Colorado over Christmas. Her daughter Trish was a single mom in her early 40's with five girls ranging in age from six to twenty. All of them would become a big part of my new family! Gerry planned for the three of us go to a nice restaurant in Fort Lauderdale to celebrate my one-year anniversary of being sober. Trish was in the car when Gerry picked me up at the Faith Farm.

As God would have it, the evening was certainly blessed. All three of us were comfortable, and our conversations were smooth. Trish saw my new tattoo with Jesus over Holly and thought it was such a nice idea. Very happy for her mom and me, Trish flew back to Utah, leaving us with thoughts of having had a lovely night that we'll always remember. Thank you, Jesus.

Following Gerry's daughter's visit came an email from Gerry's grandsons who were nine and eleven years old at that time. Gerry called me on a beautiful November day while I was still teaching and working at the Faith Farm to tell me about the email that said,

> "Grandma, Ben is doing ok. He won't be back in school until next week though. I got your letter with the picture of Grampa Tony in it. I hope you guys are doing ok. Please forward this to Grampa Tony. Love, Jack. Grandpa Tony, Grandma has probably already told you about me and my brother Ben. I have a couple questions:
> 1. What would you like me and my brother to call you?
> 2. What are your interests?
> I hope I get to meet you soon. Your new grandson, Jack"

That email blew me away. That night I called Jack and Ben. First, we talked about what to call me. My daughter Holly used to call my father "Gramps," so I suggested that. I was overwhelmed with love from Jack, and I hadn't even met him yet! That's God! Then, we talked about my hobbies, like old cars, and soon we got onto the subject of God and the Bible and how I'm learning about it where I'm living. I told him I was in a Christian program, and he understood that. I told him I was looking forward to Christmas when we would meet each other. He and his brother were so excited. God was giving me a new family, and soon I'd be meeting them. The best part of God's love story between us is that I was becoming the man He intended me to be—the man He created! He blessed me with a beautiful Christian woman who wanted to be my wife and wanted to give me a new family. I didn't deserve this after all I had done, but God saw it differently. I was walking with Him. He was with me to show everyone at the Faith Farm, Calvary Chapel, and Celebrate Recovery that there is hope for everyone!

We flew into Colorado three days before Christmas in 2013 and met Gerry's son, daughter-in-law, and their sons, Jack and Ben, Gerry's grandchildren. The ski house where we were staying was so beautiful that my insides were asking my outsides if this was real! I couldn't believe what was happening! The love that Gerry's family showed me was beyond what I had ever experienced!

Christmas brought back so many memories! We had the seven fishes Christmas Eve—the same as I had known as a child when my mother made those dishes! Gerry made two huge trays of lasagna for Christmas Day, and Gerry's daughter-in-law's mom and dad joined us for Christmas. What a wonderful week we had with everyone there. My life was being directed by the Holy Spirit, and I loved everything about my new life walking with God. I was experiencing a peace on earth that I never knew existed!

After that week, we flew to Utah to visit Gerry's daughter Trish and her five girls. What a beautiful time doing whatever we were doing—watching movies, shopping, making meals, and going to restaurants. I was learning how to live life the right way. God's way! My fears were quieted knowing that God had me in the real spiritual realm. Everyone was looking forward to 2014, a year of everything new with God!

The time came for us to go back to Florida. We didn't want to leave, and the family didn't want us to leave, but both of us were expected back. I was starting a new year with the guys at Faith Farm, and Gerry was working and sponsoring women in Alcoholics Anonymous.

After meeting her family and being accepted, we both knew that we had to set a date for our wedding, believing God had put us together and given us great purpose as a married couple. We talked and prayed about the where and when for our wedding.

In the meantime, the Faith Farm celebrated its annual Homecoming in February. All three Faith Farms, the one in Fort Lauderdale where I was, another one in Boynton Beach, FL, and another one in Lake Okeechobee, FL, participated in the all-day event under an enormous circus tent in Boynton Beach. There were softball games, fishing in the lake, worship bands, and testimonies from graduates for the 1,500 people who attended. At this, my first Homecoming event ever, Pastor Doug Lidwell offered to line up the same tent for our wedding at the Faith Farm in Fort Lauderdale once we decided on the date! That wouldn't be for a while because Gerry and I both wanted to wait until her whole family was free to come to Florida, and that would be after school ended, most likely in the summer.

Finally, our wedding date was set for July 5, 2014. Pastor Douglas gave us a workbook titled *Love and Respect* to counsel us before we were married. I'd been in the recovery program for seventeen months and I was still amazed to be sober and saved! I love having a personal relationship with my Lord and Savior, Jesus Christ. I'd been studying the Bible and learning to be the head of the household, the husband God wants me to be to Gerry, and how to honor my beautiful, soon-to-be wife. Gerry and I studied *Love and Respect* together. We saw each other on Wednesdays at church. I continued to live, teach, and work at the Faith Farm with Stu Lane and another brother in Christ named Andrew, an Irish guy who played a guitar in the worship band and had the same last name as Gerry. We'd become *goombahs*.

Still, a few other things had to be settled before Gerry and I could get married. We knew we couldn't get married at Saint Paul's Catholic Church because my first marriage hadn't been annulled, but that was handled. It seems that my second wife Michole divorced me in 2004 while I was on the road driving trucks cross-country. I never saw the paperwork for the divorce because it went to the house that was listed as my residence on my restraining order. My mother was gone. My dad knew about Michole's mission to divorce me, but what could he do? He was in hospice. Another thing that had to be dealt with was coming clean with the child support that I hadn't paid since 2003 when I was slapped with $450 a week! I assumed that my driver's license was still valid. I was arrested for a DUI in 2003, but a friend in Indiana checked to see if my license was still good in 2004, and it was still okay then. I wasn't sure when my license had been suspended, but apparently it had been.

To start the process, I called the Bergen County Courthouse in New Jersey who ordered me to pay child support when I was in survival mode becoming homeless and living on drugs and alcohol. I told my testimony to the woman who answered the phone. She wanted to help, I thought. She gave me her personal phone number after we spoke for about three hours. Holly was now sixteen, and, as I understood the restraining order, I still could not speak with her or visit her until she was eighteen. I didn't know where she and Michole were living, and their phone numbers, of course, had changed. The woman from the county courthouse advised me to send $1,000 and make a trip to New Jersey in person for an upcoming Child Support Amnesty Week, saying the court will waive my arrest warrant and come to an agreement for weekly support payments if I did so. Gerry had a friend who was an airline stewardess who could get me a buddy pass to fly to New Jersey. I was going to give them $500, make an agreement to pay, and return to the Faith Farm. But God had a different plan.

About three days before I was supposed to leave, the woman from the courthouse called me and told me that I didn't have to make the trip to New Jersey if I could wire $1,000 overnight to the support agency. The process would begin as soon as the payment reached the office, and I wouldn't have to go there in person! We sent the money to the support agency. Two days later I was contacted that the agency had all my information, and about four days later, a large envelope came to me. Inside was a letter from the judge saying that my arrest warrant was waived, along with paperwork to get my driver's license revalidated. All of this happened a week before Gerry and I were planning to get married. Two days before our wedding, when I went to the DMV to get my Florida driver's license, the clerk told me that there was a problem with my license. He didn't know exactly what it was, but he gave me my license anyway and advised us to seek a lawyer to find out what the problem was. Gerry called a friend who was a lawyer to investigate. Turns out, the warrant for my arrest was for grand theft! Remember that car lot that Greg and the guys and I were paid to haul trash from to satisfy Code Enforcement? The dealership where we were paid to haul away anything inside and outside the four dumpsters? Well, the son of the owner initiated the warrant saying that I stole that air conditioner!

The owner of the dealership happened to go to Gerry's church, so just before our wedding, Gerry paid him a visit to tell him about the warrant, the wedding, and our honeymoon. The owner was totally embarrassed by what had happened. He knew the warrant was a mistake and that Greg's landscaping had taken responsibility by paying the dealership $2,500 for the "mistake." He wrote a letter to that effect, had it notarized, and gave it to Gerry. The lawyer advised us to go ahead with the honeymoon cruise because there was no way I could turn myself in or show the letter to a judge—no way to settle the matter that holiday weekend before the cruise. Glen, the attorney, told Gerry I'd most likely be arrested soon. The odd thing to me was, the police *knew* where I was when I was living at the Faith Farm making $100 a week. Prior to that, in February, I started sending $50 a week to the woman from the Bergen County courthouse who deposited the money into my child support account. I believe she was one of God's angels sent to help me. There are people on earth, I truly believe, who appear human like us, but they are God's angels who lead us out of darkness! The Bible tells us in Hebrews 13:2 that we may be entertaining angels without knowing it,

> "This is God's universe, and He does things His way. You
> may have a better way, but you don't have a universe."
> Dr. J. Vernon McGee (1904–1988)

Chapter 17

Lookin' Up

THE PLANS FOR OUR three-day wedding event were in place! All five of Gerry's sisters and friends would be staying at a hotel in Deerfield Beach to experience a July Fourth barbeque with tents, lots of food, and fun! Andrew Curran, my *goombah*, would be there with our mutual friend Gary and Pastor Douglas' son, Jeremiah, to play Christian music on the beach before the fireworks. Then, Gerry would go back to her condo with some of her grandchildren. Seven grandchildren would be in our wedding party the next day. Our daughter would be our Maid of Honor and our son, Richard, would give his mom to me. My long-time friend Frankie would be my Best Man. Four guys from Faith Farm's Maintenance Department would stand with me as well as others from Celebrate Recovery at Calvary Chapel. Pastor Douglas' daughter Dallas and his other son, John David, would be in our wedding party too.

A banquet would be set up for the reception in Fellowship Hall, complete with decorations, tables for about two hundred people, a disco ball, lights, a sound system for a disc jockey, and plenty of food! The plan for Sunday would be to go to a pool party at Gerry's girlfriend's clubhouse! Then, Gerry and I would go on a honeymoon cruise to Roatan-Cozumel, Mexico, on Royal Caribbean's "Vision of the Seas." All of this turned out to be over-the-top for me! I believe God put all the plans together, so I give Him all the praise!

This cruise, my first one ever, even offered side excursions! Gerry picked a side trip that put us into an underwater glass boat that lowered us into the domain of all kinds of fish gaping at us among coral reefs and underwater plants that I never knew existed! Wow. I was seeing God's vibrant underwater creation from a new and very wide-eyed perspective!

On a land excursion that I picked, we took four-wheel motorcycles through the jungle! This was new to Gerry. She'd never been on a four-wheeler! We put on helmets and rode behind our guide. Gerry drove in the middle.

Honeymoon jungle excursion!

The ride was treacherous. Lots of rocks, boulders, tight paths, quick turns, and much to get stuck in, and it wasn't long before Gerry's vehicle was sinking in mud! She gunned it, lost control of the steering, and flew off the four-wheeler just before it hit a tree! The bike almost landed on top of her! I was freaking out, but Gerry got up, more concerned about the bike than about herself. We rolled the bike upright with the help of the guide, and when Gerry told him how sorry she was about breaking his "bicycle," I lost it!

"I'm sorry I broke your bicycle!"

I couldn't believe she said that! So innocent! I had to laugh even though it wasn't funny! God was with us. Gerry wasn't seriously hurt. Thank you, LORD! I told her to climb onto my four-wheeler, and we'd ride back to the camp, but she insisted she was okay, and said, "Let's go!" When we got back to the camp, Gerry took a dip in the ocean thinking that the salt water would be good for her scrapes and cuts. She had a big bruise on her hip which the ship's doctor looked at once we got back onboard. Thank God nothing was broken! That evening, the ship's doctor called our room to make sure Gerry had everything she needed. Cool. God was always looking out for my bride and me!

A week later, I was back at the Faith Farm speaking at a morning chapel service. It was time for me to tell the guys that I'd be leaving the Farm so I could start my new life with Gerry. I gave my testimony and repeated how God helped me change into His new creation at the Farm.

Our wedding

"Do not conform to the pattern of this world, but be transformed by the renewing of your mind. Then you will be able to test and approve what God's will is—his good, pleasing and perfect will." Romans 12:2 NIV

Our wedding party

"Instead of your shame you will receive a double portion, and instead of disgrace you will rejoice in your inheritance. And so you will inherit a double portion in your land, and everlasting joy will be yours." Isaiah 61:7 NIV

Chapter 18

The Catch of the Day

OUR LUXURIOUS FLOATING PALACE, the "Vision of the Seas," slipped into Port Everglades after our most wonderful Caribbean honeymoon cruise! Our bags were packed, we settled our bill, checked the safe, and closed our cabin door for the last time. We were told to hold onto our personal keycards because at the exit, Security required each of us to put our keycard into a turnstyle to register our final departure.

When I slid my keycard into the slot, a siren went off, red and yellow lights were flashing all over the place, and a clanging bell threw everyone's attention right to me as if I'd just won the Showcase Showdown on The Price is Right! Security officers were coming toward me advising me not to be alarmed because this was simply a random luggage check. Really? Gerry and I were escorted through the baggage area and into two separate rooms where Gerry dug the notarized letter out of her bag and told Security that she was aware of the warrant and that it was a mistake. She explained the circumstances and showed Security the letter from the owner of the dealership. Security hoped Gerry would understand that they couldn't do anything about the letter—that would be for a judge to decide. I was escorted off the cruise ship where I met the Broward Sheriff and several police officers in person. They didn't handcuff me in front of Gerry; they simply escorted me to the back seat of a police car. They told Gerry that if she brought $1,000 to the station, I could be bonded out that day. Police were respectful. They saw the notarized letter from the dealership, but couldn't do anything other than what they were sent to do—take me to jail. Gerry's car was parked at the dock, so she was free to drive home with our luggage. I was thanking God all the way to jail that they didn't arrest me before our amazing cruise! Some things just can't be taken away!

I was put into a holding pod (place of detention) with a bunch of other guys who mostly were there for drug violations. This was an opportunity for me to tell them my testimony—how I wound up at the Faith Farm, learned about Jesus, got saved, and just got back from the most amazing honeymoon with my bride. They were listening because they needed and wanted help. Besides that, they couldn't go anywhere else. Praying with them gave them hope and showed me how God continues to reach others through our personal experiences with Him. No one can dispute what happened to me. I thank God every time I'm able to share my story and, thereby, give hope to someone else who needs a good dose of it. Gerry paid the bail, and at three o'clock in the morning, I was free to leave the jail.

A court date was set. We showed up with our lawyer, and for five or six times our case was postponed for one reason or another. Finally, the judge saw the notarized letter given to Gerry by the owner of the dealership, and the case was thrown out of court. No prosecution. I felt God was with me the whole time. I was thinking about the Apostle Paul when he was in jail singing praises with his friend Silas. The Bible says a believer can talk with God day or night no matter where the location is or what the circumstances are. I took advantage of that in jail. One of the inmates prayed sincerely to receive Jesus, and myriads of angels sang all over Heaven all night long!

Chapter 19

Ob-la-di, Ob-la-da

IN TWO YEARS GOD had transformed my life at the Faith Farm. I was ready to start my new life as a new man, a new husband to Gerry, a new father to my stepson and stepdaughter, a new grandfather to five girls and two boys in a home with my wife Gerry. As promised, God poured blessings on me daily.

> *"For I know the plans I have for you, declares the LORD, plans to prosper you and not to harm you, plans to give you hope and a future."* Jeremiah 29:11 NIV

Starting over in a new home was an adjustment for Gerry and me. We were in a nice bedroom without two hundred other men making noises. I was waking up sober beside a beautiful woman instead of being sick after fighting with demons all night. Reality set in quickly when I realized Gerry was off to work, and I was sitting in my home alone. I knew I needed to find work right away because when I'm working, there's less chance for the adversary to grab my ear and tell me how one little drink to celebrate the victory is okay. He's so good at distorting the truth! He makes sounds like, "Jesus drank, so . . ."

Prayer and the Word of God are my best defenses against evil, I've learned. So, I prayed and started to re-read all my homework from the Faith Farm. Then, I stepped out and started to volunteer with whatever work came my way. That day, Gerry's friend called her at work, and when Gerry told her friend that I wasn't at the Faith Farm anymore, the friend asked Gerry if I would be interested in painting their condo in Florida. She and her husband were snowbirds from Indiana. The friend and her husband offered to send me gift cards to cash at the Home Depot for the paint and other supplies, including window treatments. God is so good! Almost immediately my work at the condo began while I was still volunteering at the Faith Farm church and at Saint Paul's. My life was starting to take shape again, this time in a one-true Godly way.

Not quite two months after Gerry and I were married, a friend named Gary, who went through recovery at the Faith Farm with me, called from northern Florida to tell me that he had backslidden and needed help. We talked, and soon Gary moved into our spare bedroom. We brought Gary to Celebrate Recovery, and joined the Twelve-Step class with him. We worked on the recovery steps together, and Gary worked alongside me at the condo. He had gone to college to become a jet mechanic! He had sent out a number of resumes, but didn't have any responses. However, another girlfriend of Gerry, the airline stewardess who offered to give me a buddy pass to fly to New Jersey to address my delinquent child support, inherited her mother's condo after her mom died.

When we finished both condos, Gary got a call from an old contractor boss of his named Joe who told him he had a job and needed his help. Gary asked if I could come along, and Joe told him, "Yes, bring him. The job is in Davie, Florida. I'll pay you $75 a day." It was doing condo demo and rebuilding, something we were good at—in fact, Joe was so happy with our work that he upped the pay to $20 an hour. Soon, only Gary and I were working; the boss went to do other things. But, Gary was still hoping to return to working as a jet mechanic. His drug testing was clean. Gerry told him to dress up with jeans, a nice shirt, and his cowboy boots (that he always wore) and go to the Fort Lauderdale Executive Airport. She advised him to go into the hangars to see if anyone was looking for an "old school" jet mechanic. How amazing! Gary was hired in the first hangar!

A week later, Gary started as a jet mechanic, and Joe and I stayed behind to finish the condos. We plugged along, finished the condos in January of 2015, and I became Joe's partner in a contracting business. At about this time a Calvary Chapel church in Wilton Manors was having a work day at the school, so Joe and I volunteered to help. I found out then that Joe, my partner, had a problem with drugs and alcohol. Mutual friends told me that he would show up high or hung over from the night before, and that he was missing days at work. I tried to help him. We worked with a bunch of guys that day, and that's when I met a guy named David who was a wallpaper hanger. What a nice surprise. I told him how my father taught me to paint and hang wallpaper, and I was glad when David gave me his phone number. We worked together that day and had a great time.

Joe came to Celebrate Recovery with Gary and me, but didn't go through the Twelve-Steps. Gary was doing okay as a jet mechanic, and before long, the work that Joe and I were doing started to slow down. I told Joe I wanted to do everything the right way by getting a company name, but he'd had trouble with the IRS and couldn't do it. Then, in the mail I got another suspension of my driver's license for not paying enough child support! We hired a lawyer and went to court again. The judge told me I needed a legitimate job, not just working come-what-may jobs with a friend because for the ten years that I was out of the child support system, I owed $150,000 in child support! The deal was, I could keep my driver's license if I paid $214 a week.

I wanted to fulfill my child support obligation. I needed my driver's license and I needed a reliable, legitimate job! God knew every detail because He showed up again. I left the court with my driver's license backed up by a promise to start paying the required funds. I believe God softened the judge's heart toward me.

The first person I called after being in court that day was Joe to tell him that I wouldn't be working with him anymore. He started screaming at me on the phone, so I hung up and didn't answer even though he kept calling. Then, finally, when I answered the phone, Joe wasn't on the other end; the caller was David, the wallpaper hanger who remembered me from the work day in Wilton Manors. David wondered if I was still working with Joe and asked me if I was looking for steady work. Then, he added, "The Holy Spirit was all over me in church on Sunday to call you, and I couldn't get 'Call Tony. Call Tony' out of my head since then. So, I'm calling you!"

I told him what happened in court and about my split with Joe. David's timing couldn't have been better! If you've ever been afraid that you might lose your job, you know how scary it can be. Psalm 6 says, *"Be gracious to me, O LORD, for I am languishing. O LORD, heal me, for my bones are shaking with terror."* God knew where I was, and He had a plan!

When David asked if I'd go to Jupiter, Florida, to work with him, I told him without hesitating that I'd go to Mars if that's what he needed! He asked for my address and told me he'd pick me up the next day at six in the morning. Jupiter was one hour from Deerfield where Gerry and I were living, so David and I drove to Jupiter the next morning and had a great conversation all the way! Thank you, LORD! Thank you! Thank you! Thank you!

We pulled into a strip mall in Jupiter that had six store fronts with a huge office in the back that was occupied by yoga, pilates, and gymnastics with different teachers all day. Another office was used by Southeast Certified Construction. Three others were ready to rent. I realized right away that I'd need a lift to paint the tall peaks and dormers. Painting this building inside and out would take me a year, I told David. He said that would be okay and advised me to keep track of my hours. I'd be paid $25 an hour at the end of each week. From there we drove to a paint store where David set up a charge account for supplies. "I'll work the first week with you 'til you get comfortable. Then you'll be on your own." David and I started working together in March of 2015. Our friendship was what I needed. David was a stable believer. Working there meant getting myself up at 4 a.m., leaving the house by five o'clock and beating the traffic to get to the site by 6 a.m. These were some of the most beautiful, uplifting drives of my life because I watched God painting a new sky every morning at sunrise.

One day a man named Kevin came into the building and introduced himself as the owner of the building and the owner of Southeast Certified Construction. He had been speaking with David, he said, and asked me to stop what I was doing at the moment and go with him. He wanted to show me something. On that Friday afternoon, after I packed up, I rode with Kevin to a condo complex in Palm Beach across the bay from Singer Island. We took the elevator to a condo that Kevin wanted to gut and rebuild on the twenty-fifth floor! And, Kevin wanted me to run the operation as a supervisor. Not a small job! But, by God's grace, I had the experience and the know-how to do it right. We ripped out walls, installed a new kitchen and two new bathrooms, replaced sheetrock, plumbing, and wiring. Then David and I painted and wallpapered the unit. I was there for about two months before going back to the strip mall to finish the work there. And, that's when David and Kevin approached me while I was working to inform me that I couldn't work for them anymore! Did I do something wrong? Was I being fired? They answered me with this: "We're not firing you! You need to start your own company and work *with* us not *for* us!"

I had the income to set up what was needed to become a licensed entity. David and Gerry helped me organize my paperwork. On May 18, 2015, God gave me my own licensed and insured company, Bada Bing Handyman LLC. My work started with David's wallpapering company and Kevin's Southeast Certified Construction. The work quickly expanded to South Miami covering hotels, ballrooms, and businesses. God kept pouring His blessings on me in my new life, as well as on David's and Kevin's lives! David's brother-in-law owned and operated a construction and painting company—another open door for me. Upperclassmen and graduates from the Faith Farm were able to work on projects. God was using me as I'd asked Him to do!

> *"And my God will supply every need of yours according to His riches in Glory in Christ Jesus."* Philippians 4:19

Chapter 20

Stop, Look, and Listen!

"You have to be very careful if you don't know where you are going, because you might not get there."

Yogi Berra

After finishing the Twelve-Step program at Celebrate Recovery at Calvary Chapel, I was approached by my good friend Jonathan, the leader of Celebrate Recovery at that time, to work alongside someone who wanted to learn how to teach the program. "How do you know I can teach?" I asked. Jonathan said he knew that I taught at the Faith Farm and asked me to choose a day to teach so he could find a classroom for me. I remembered Stu Lane telling me on his deathbed that as long as he stayed in the classroom, he never drank or did drugs again. That was for thirty years! Stu encouraged me even more by saying, "God has anointed you to teach!" I took this as a hug from God.

> *"I will instruct you and teach you in the way you should go; I will counsel you with my loving eye on you."*
> Psalm 32:8 NIV

My class began in September of 2015. No sooner than that, Jonathan told me there was a shortage of leaders for New Believers.

I remembered becoming a new believer when I went to the altar on Christmas Eve in 2012 and gave my life to the Lord. I asked Him then to use me to benefit as many lives as possible with the hope that only He has to offer before my time comes to leave this planet. The realizaiton of seeing a full circle as a leader serving others brought me a deep sense of gratitude.

My new ministry, The Armor of God, began as I worked with Calvary Chapel teaching the Twelve-Steps in Celebrate Recovery, still maintaining contact with the men at the Faith Farm, even some of the ones who had graduated with me. One of those men was my friend Jake who was there the day I arrived at the Farm. He was one of the only people I'd ever met who was bigger than I was! He introduced himself as "Big Jake" and offered to help me in any way. Apparently, he came back to the Faith Farm after graduating because he had started using drugs again. I was glad that he'd come back, and we maintained a close relationship. My life was busy and very good.

One evening in April of 2016, my cell phone started vibrating on my belt while I was teaching my class at Calvary Chapel. I glanced at the number and saw that the person trying to reach me was Pastor Douglas from the Faith Farm. Didn't he know that I was teaching a class and couldn't answer my phone? I disconnected the call, but it kept coming back every three minutes. Finally, I asked my co-facilitator to take the class while I excused myself and went into the hallway to see what was so urgent. "We found Jake in the bathroom with a needle still in his arm. Come as soon as you can," Pastor Douglas quietly told me.

My co-facilitator taught the remainder of my class, and by the time I got to the Faith Farm, the ambulance was leaving with Jake who was barely alive, they told me. The police had already cordoned off Jake's apartment. Some of us went through the three floors of dorms looking for any evidence that would help the investigation. One of my friends had Jake's phone. Clearly, the name of the guy who sold and delivered the stuff was listed on the recent texts exposing the whole transaction. The seller was a guy who had graduated a year ago. Big Jake who gave his life to Christ and was baptized before I was—Big Jake, the great encourager who made me feel comfortable on my awkward first day at the Faith Farm! No! How terribly sad! What *any* of us would have given to replay and change the hours before Jake contacted that dealer!

After Jake's memorial service, his body was shipped back to Tennessee where he was born. His wife had divorced him. His daughter was only four years old. Jake's death may have been accidental, but what does that matter even now?

There are a lot of sad stories out of the Faith Farm and other programs. Losing Big Jake was the first overdose that devastated me. I was his friend and his sponsor! I had no way of knowing that he'd started using again! And, at that point, I had no way of knowing that soon after Jake's death, the life of my other wonderful, animated friend JoJo, the nearly professional baseball player who was my classmate and fellow worker at the Faith Farm—my friend who heard about Celebrate Recovery through a customer and invited me to go with him to Calvary Chapel—a sweet guy who was married with four children and whose tattoo on his arm read "Serenity"—would end suddenly with an overdose too!

These fatal overdoses ignited an anger inside me that stirred up a personal war on addiction. Heartaches bring hard lessons. Using drugs is Russian Roulette. We must learn to stand strong day-by-day against the enemy who destroys lives. To do that, we have to live in recovery around-the-clock in our drug-free community, going to meetings, staying with programs, studying the Bible, praying a lot, and being intentional about recovery! And, we must remember that God is love. He heals and restores, so it's vital for us to stay close to Him. Satan, on the other hand, is described as the thief who *"comes only to steal and kill and destroy; I (Jesus) have come that they may have life, and have it to the full."* John 10:10 NIV The Bible refers to Satan as the father of all lies, and his greatest lie is that he doesn't exist! Who doesn't know this? Wake up now if you don't know this!

God has given each us free will. A person can follow the teaching of a recovery program or go back to using with a huge risk of dying. I was not, by any means, going back to that dark place where I struggled for forty years! I continue to fight with all the tools I got from the Faith Farm to stay sober and alert.

I look at all the guys from the past who did not make it as a teaching to me not to return to my old ways. God gave me a second chance at the Faith Farm with all the tools, such as Celebrate Recovery, even leadership with New Believers at Calvary Chapel, and in the community through my handyman business to move forward on a foundation that allows me to serve Him alongside the amazing Family of God.

God showed up every day! Why? Because every morning I invited Him into my day one-day-at-a-time. God goes where He is invited. He's not pushy. Revelation 3:20 KJV reads: *"Behold, I stand at the door and knock. If anyone hears my voice and opens the door, I will come into him and eat with him, and he with me."* So, every day, I invite Him to breakfast, to my ten o'clock break, then to lunch, dinner, and every other chance I have to lean on Him! *"Be strong and courageous,"* the Bible says in Deuteronomy 31:6 NIV *"Do not be afraid or terrified because of them, for the LORD your God goes with you; he will never leave you nor forsake you."* I lean on Him day and night. He helps me survive in this crazy world. He is my sanity! God wants to live through me to show His light.

"Call to me," my Creator says in Jeremiah 33:3 NIV, *"and I will answer you and tell you great and unsearchable things you do not know."*

I am forever grateful to be available to God, and I love when He shows me things I don't know anything about or surprises me with a desire that's deep in my heart. One of those desires was to have contact with my daughter Holly again. In 2014, my friend Gary showed me how Facebook worked, and when I found out that people were finding friends from the past, I started praying that God would use Facebook to help me find my daughter Holly. In the beginning of 2017, God answered my prayer; I saw Holly's name on Facebook! Before trying to contact her, I met with my pastor who agreed with what Gerry had suggested, that is, writing a letter of amends to my ex-wife Michole. Although I agreed to write the letter, I didn't have any idea where to send it. The miracle to me is, I was able to read all of Holly's Facebook pages from when she was about thirteen years old without being accepted as a friend! Only God could have done that! And, on one of her pages, she was holding up a letter with her address written on it! The shame and guilt of what I had done to her and her mother overwhelmed me, especially when I read that Holly was struggling with her identity and that her mom had married a guy from Alcoholics Anonymous in 2004 right after my restraining order took effect. For seven years or so, I knew the guy who became Holly's stepdad!

Without my praying before writing every sentence, the letter of amends to Holly's mom would not have happened. Finally, I signed it and sent it. Shortly afterward, Holly and I started to converse on Facebook. Then we started to talk on the phone. Holly told me that her mom never talked bad about me to her, and I was relieved about that. Holly was enrolled at Temple University to become a nurse, and that made me so proud of her! I felt God's desire to repair our relationship.

In 2017 Holly told me she would be coming to Florida to see Zeyde, her grandfather, who was living in a community about ten minutes from where I was living! How amazing is that? Holly and I set up a meeting to have lunch on Sunday, July 3rd, at a popular local diner. From my seat beside a window inside the restaurant I recognized her! Fourteen years had passed since I'd seen the blond, curly-headed little girl I missed so much! Seeing her coming across the parking lot with my ex-father-in-law left me speechless and breathless! She was tall and beautiful! Her hair was pulled back. That billboard smile was unmistakably hers!

We recognized each other immediately, so I walked up to her, hugged her, and started to cry, telling her that I loved her. She hugged me back, we held each other tight, and I could feel her trembling in my arms. Her grandfather said hello. I showed him respect, but didn't look to get anything back after what I had done to his daughter and granddaughter. I took Holly's hands in mine and locked eyes with her. That's when she told me she had a few questions. "Okay, go ahead, Holly," I said, shaking in my boots. She looked at me and said, "When we were in the police station,

I looked up at you and you looked down at me and said, 'Don't worry, Holly, I'll be home in a couple of days.'" She remembered that from when she was five years old? Apparently, she remembered it like it happened yesterday! That blew me away. My answer was, "Your mother had a restraining order, and I couldn't come home." To that, Holly said, "Okay." That was probably the lamest excuse I could have come up with, but it was true. Her question shocked me. Then she wanted to know about child support. "I saw that you got arrested. Was that for the child support? That's why you're paying it now?" I explained that the arrest was about the air conditioner mistake from the dealership and told her that I started to pay the child support when I was at the Faith Farm because I wanted to become the man God created me to be. I wanted to pay the support that I should have been paying all those years.

Holly told me her news. She said that she knew I was a minister now and that I might not agree with her or want her in my life. "I'm gay, and I have a girlfriend," she told me. I looked at her and said, "Holly, I don't judge. Who am I to judge you after what I did to you by not being there as your dad? God does the loving and the judging. I'm called to do the loving only. I love you unconditionally with whatever choices you make, Holly. I'm praying that we'll have a relationship as father and daughter, and I'll be the dad that I never was." We spent some time together—joyful to see each other; nevertheless, things that had been bothering her for years needed to be answered. We talked over lunch for about an hour. Then, Zeyde took a nice picture of us together, Holly gave me her phone number, and we became friends on Facebook.

On that Fourth of July weekend, Gerry and I were about to celebrate our anniversary on July 5th with Trish and two of our grandchildren who wanted to celebrate with us. Holly met us on the beach. I shared my testimony with her and was feeling good about our relationship. She listened and was glad that I was sober. There were no questions about the Faith Farm, but I could sense that our delayed relationship was beginning to grow. Holly left. The next day Gerry and I celebrated our third anniversary with our family. God is so good. His Word continues to encourage and delight me daily through His Word :*"The LORD your God has blessed you in all the work of your hands. He has watched over your journey through this vast wilderness. These forty years (emphasis mine) the LORD your God has been with you, and you have not lacked anything."* Deuteronomy 2:7 NIV

I'm looking at my life and God's promises in Matthew 7:7,

"Ask and it will be given to you; seek, and you will find; knock and the door will be opened to you." NIV

Chapter 21

Choose Life

IN 2018, I CELEBRATED my sixty-first birthday sober and over-whelmed by God's goodness, mercy, and grace. Contact with my daughter Holly and her girlfriend happened over Christmas in 2017, my business and ministries were growing, and God was the center of my marriage to Gerry and my new family. Wow! God had really saved my life and turned everything around for me!

At the end of March, I got a phone call from my Aunt Paula, my mother's little sister—my aunt who was more like a sister to me because she was only six years older than I was! We grew up together! She got my phone number from my mother's best friend Betty after I called her from the Faith Farm. Betty's phone number was the only working number that I could find in a little book that had been buried in my belongings. I don't know how the word got back to Betty that I had died of a brain aneurism, but she was glad to hear that I was alive and in recovery in Florida. The call from my Aunt Paula came to me while I was in a Celebrate Recovery class. Even though I hadn't heard from her for years, her voice sounded the same!

"How are you, Anthony?"

"I'm sober and blessed. How are you?"

"Not good. I have stage four lung cancer like your mom had—and some brain tumors."

We prayed. I consoled her, and we talked about old times that made both of us laugh. I read this scripture to her before our call ended: *"Peace I leave with you; my peace I give you. I do not give to you as the world gives. Do not let your hearts be troubled and do not be afraid."* John 14:27 NIV

I started to call her every day, and soon Gerry and I booked a flight to New Jersey to spend the weekend with my Aunt Paula. Then, the greatest thing happened! The three of us were talking about God when I told my Aunt Paula that I brought some oil with me and wanted to pray a healing prayer on her. We talked about her surrendering her life to the Lord and getting ready for Heaven. She was willing, so we prayed the sinner's prayer with her and anointed her with oil while asking God for her healing. The joy that only the Holy Spirit can give filled the room and swept all fears, doubts, and concerns away from us! Lots of tears, but they were happy ones, as we reminisced what we could remember. Aunt Paula relived the day I was born and all my birthdays! We ate some great Italian food, and Gerry got to hear all about how Aunt Paula and I grew up together. FUN! That weekend was something we all needed!

Easter was about to happen when we got back to Fort Lauderdale, so we decided to celebrate with family and friends, including friends who didn't have families. One of those was a young guy named Tommy who adopted me as his "spiritual father" in 2014 while he was in Celebrate Recovery. On Father's Day he always sent me a card for sponsoring him through the Twelve-Steps. We'd spent a lot of time together in and outside of church. Sadly, not long after he graduated from the Twelve-Step program, he started to drink and use pills again, so I got him into the Faith Farm where he did well. He graduated and got a job, so I was looking forward to spending more time with him.

Seeing Tommy wasn't what I expected at all. He showed up high, and during the dinner, he started acting crazy, cursing and carrying on, so eventually I took him outside for a chat because there were a lot of other people present. I found out he'd been thrown out of the Faith Farm the week before because he was drinking. Tommy told me that he was okay and started to walk toward his scooter. "Are you driving that?" I nodded toward his scooter. He said he was. I asked him to leave the scooter at my house and let me drive him home, but he started fighting me, insisting that he was okay. "Call me tomorrow," I said hoping he heard me and feeling that I should have done more for him as he revved up and flew off. "I want you to get back into the Farm!"

We all have choices, and, sadly, some of our choices aren't the best for us. Tommy didn't call me, but Pastor Douglas' wife called me a few days later to tell me that Tommy had been in a serious car accident. A retired policeman who knew Tommy and me from Calvary Chapel was the officer who responded to that emergency call. Apparently, all traffic was stopped because the bridge was up on the 14th Street Causeway in Pompano that night. Tommy was high and not wearing a helmet when he drove his scooter full-speed into a car on the Causeway. He died at the scene of head trauma. His pockets were full of drugs. He was the only "son" I had ever known, and I was shaken by his death.

We can't force good choices on people who don't want them. The Bible urges us to *"Be alert and of sober mind. Your enemy the devil prowls around like a roaring lion looking for someone to devour. Resist him, standing firm in the faith, because you know that the family of believers throughout the world is undergoing the same kind of sufferings."* 1 Peter 5:8, 9 NIV

Another phone call came from my screaming Aunt Paula, "Anthony! Is Gerry with you?" She was. "Am I on speaker?" Aunt Paula had news: The doctors had been doing MRI's, and that day, when she went to get radiation on her brain, they told her that the tumors in her head were GONE!! No radiation would be needed!! She said the prayers worked—we assured her it was all God; Gerry and I only did what we were told to do, that is, believe and pray. I believe Jesus was giving my aunt and Gerry and me more time together. Aunt Paula was able to drive again, so she went back to work at the monument company. We kept in touch on Facebook to talk about God, the Bible, my testimony, my dark side, and my making amends with people I'd hurt. My aunt said she felt so bad about turning her back on me, but I told her she had to do it because I hadn't hit bottom yet, so by turning her back on me, she actually helped save my life.

Gerry and I spent Christmas that year with my Aunt Paula. What a blessing to all of us to be together shopping, eating, and reminiscing. We bought my aunt a leatherbound, name-engraved Bible accompanied by a "Bada Bing Handyman" shirt and some warm socks. We made up for a lot of the fifty years of joy that we thought we had lost! On that Christmas God brought another close relative back into my life by way of Facebook—my cousin Danny Cass, the son of my godfather Joey Cass who was the drummer for the Four Seasons so many years ago. He was living in California, following in his father's footsteps as a drummer. We reconnected and caught up with our past. God was bringing my family back into my life! Although God was speaking to the children of Zion in the book of Joel in the Bible, I felt His promise was for me, as well, *"And I will restore to you the years that the locust hath eaten—"* Joel 2:25 KJV

More events occurred in 2019 verifying God's promise to restore my life. As 2019 began, my business and ministries were doing well. I continued teaching at Celebrate Recovery and New Believers when I was told that I had been nominated by my good friend Jonathan who led Celebrate Recovery to become a deacon at Calvary Chapel. Deacon and Elder Training was required for me to learn the responsibilities according to the Bible. On May 8, 2019, I was prayed in as a deacon of Calvary Chapel in Fort Lauderdale. Many ministerial duties came with my new title, including baptizing believers, counseling at the altar, visiting and praying with those in hospitals and in hospice, performing memorial services, etc. What an enormous honor and privilege it became for me to be ordained as a deacon!

In June, Gerry and I flew to Indiana to meet our first great-granddaughter! Never had I thought that such a blessing would happen to me! God is with me day and night! Thank you, Heavenly Father, for sparing my life and showing me a new life greater than what I could have asked for or imagined!

"For I know the plans I have for you," declares the LORD, plans to prosper you and not to harm you, plans to give you hope and a future." Jeremiah 29:11 NIV

In July of 2019, Gerry and I went to our first Celebrate Recovery Summit in Tennessee. Calvary Chapel provided four vans for us to drive to Tennessee with Jonathan and other CR leaders. We worshiped with 5,000 other believers! There is nothing like being with the Family of God! That felt like Jesus spiritually feeding the five thousand, and we were blessed and privileged to be listening to great speakers for three days. Some of the speakers taught powerful messages while others gave their jaw-dropping testimonies of how they were so miraculously brought out of the deepest darkness into the light. Very Holy Spirit filled! An amazing time of revival that inspired all of us to return to Fort Lauderdale more empowered than before to spread the Gospel.

As part of my Twelve-Step recovery program, I was asked to make amends with anyone I had hurt. That included, if possible, my first wife Roseann who was living in Cape Cod where Gerry's family was planning to have a family reunion with over a hundred relatives. Roseann and her girlfriend agreed to meet us for lunch. It was the first time I had seen her in twenty-nine years! Rosey married a friend of mine who used to play darts with me when Roseann and I were married. We connected as friends, and I was able to make amends with Roseann in a pleasant setting. Only God could have orchestrated something like that! Gerry is a true minister of God to sit through my making amends to my ex-wife! What a powerful act of kindness and forgiveness! It was the first time I'd ever heard of anyone making amends to his ex-wife with his wife sitting in their presence! And, how amazing it was for Roseann to be with us and accept my words. Hearts were softened by Almighty God that day. God's grace and mercy continue to amaze me! We were reunited in true friendship that continued. Roseann was instrumental with helping my Aunt Paula. They reconnected and resumed the friendship that they had enjoyed years before, and we continued to visit them both. When Roseann's husband died, Gerry and I were there to minister to her in her grief. God's power was evident in restoring these relationships! God gave me another chance to make things right!

Every day of my life I work on my recovery. Three hundred sixty-five days a year I learn from my mistakes. I thrive on matching my walk with my talk. It's a blessing to be a sober, productive lover of God. He has protected me, provided for me, and blessed me with great purpose, which is to know Him better each day and to make Him known! He has restored my heath and my sanity! He has given me a beautiful wife and family, has restored relationships, and He has allowed me to see the wonders of His amazing creation and the truth of His Word! He has shown me that He *is* who He says He is and that His promises are always fulfilled!

> "He breaks the power of canceled sin, He sets the prisoner free; His blood can make the foulest clean, His blood availed for me." Charles Wesley, 1797–1788.

Chapter 22

Through It All

AT CHRISTMASTIME IN 2019 Gerry and I went on a ten-day cruise to Aruba, Bonaire, Curacao, and Grand Cayman Island to see beautiful things together that we had never seen before and to catch up with loving each other. God gave that to us! And, we were glad we went because we took the cruise just before the world turned upside down!

Anyone who was alive and able to communicate in 2020 knows that the COVID virus smacked the world in its face. Restaurants and stores shut down. Suppliers were soon deplete of sanitizing products. Fights for masks broke out, groceries were ordered online and handled with gloves and sanitizer, and people who thought they had the flu died instead of COVID. Social distancing became the new awareness. Many churches opted for online services as did our recovery program. Gerry and I did our recovery step studies online. The pandemic sent recovery into a tail spin. Driving on roads that usually were gridlocked and were now eerily void of traffic gave the impression that the world had stopped. Oddly enough, my handyman company kept getting busier through the pandemic! I could order my supplies online, pick them up, and pay with a credit card machine outside the front door of the store. Everyone was wearing masks, sanitizing their hands, and being extremely cautious at every turn, and yet people continued to die at an alarming rate worldwide.

The pandemic was having a profound effect on people in recovery. Our phones were ringing off the hook with news of people we knew who had relapsed. I met with Jonathan, our ministry leader, to suggest that we begin taping testimonies and running them online with our teaching. That happened.

Our house was a bit crazy. I was with a group doing Celebrate Recovery online in one room, and Gerry was online with her group at the women's meetings. Then, I'd be in the bedroom doing another virtual meeting with the men online! We also met with the people we were sponsoring throughout the week online. We watched church services online too. Besides that, I worked as a handyman all week, and my handyman business was booming! God took great care of us in every way through the pandemic; in fact, my business brought in the most money during the pandemic! I call that a miracle from God.

In March I received a letter on Facebook Messenger that my daughter Holly had changed her name to Ari with a new last name and had begun transgender hormone treatments at Christmastime, 2019, in Florida. This was all documented on her Facebook account. She said in her letter that she didn't want anything to do with me anymore. All I can do is pray for her. I love my daughter unconditionally. She wants to be called "Ari" and be addressed as "he or him," and I've asked myself so many times, "What would Jesus do?" I am called to model Jesus with my actions. I'm not God. I'm a sinner saved by grace to love others and to pray for them. In this case, I'm going to honor my son Ari's request. His letter says that he needs to move on with his life and take care of himself and his mom. I gave this to God in prayer for Ari, who never blocked me on Facebook. I've hoped he would have a change of heart to include a relationship with me before I leave this earth. In the past, I would have run to a bar or to a drug dealer or attempted suicide, but in my recovery, I pray for wisdom and understanding while running to God with my prayers. I will continue on my path of recovery, staying faithful to my God!

2020 was a kicker of a year! The pandemic picked up speed and went on killing people worldwide at an alarming rate into 2021. Almost all of us were communicating online or by phone. We missed seeing each other face-to-face, and relapses were at an all-time high. Then, Florida started opening schools and businesses in March of 2021. Another kicker of a year!

I had been working in my friend Jonathan's home. He had stepped down from leading Celebrate Recovery for a while and seemed to be chronically sick and isolating a little bit too much. Many people were still isolating because of COVID, so, Jonathan and I planned to have lunch together the following day, which was Good Friday. Getting a text or phone call at 3 a.m. almost always gives me a fast jolt. I wished the call had been part of a bad dream, but it wasn't. Instead, my God-given friend, Jonathan Dampf, who led me into recovery, encouraged me to teach and lead in Celebrate Recovery, and nominated me to become a deacon at Calvary Chapel was found unresponsive in his home—and, like *that*, Jonathan was gone! He had touched the lives of so many during his ten years of ministry which became even more evident at his standing-room only memorial. Lots of heartbreak. Friends couldn't hold back their tears that day!

In April we got word, too, that my Aunt Frannie, my Aunt Paula's sister who lived with her until she was married, died of cancer. I had not seen her for about forty years and never had the opportunity to speak or pray with her. She and my Aunt Paula always had good times together, and my Aunt Paula was distraught over Frannie's death.

In 2021, my Aunt Paula couldn't go to work anymore. She was at home alone. My ex-wife Roseann called me and told me that she had been talking with my aunt every day and felt uneasy about suddenly getting no response. We called the Hasbrook Heights Police Department to request a wellness check. After getting no answer on the phone or at the door, the police broke into Aunt Paula's condo and found her, still alive, on the floor between her bed and the wall. She spent some time in the hospital and was moved to a rehab center where she was not doing well. My cousins told me that she was asking for me, so Gerry and I flew to New Jersey to visit her. She was in bad shape, but she recognized Gerry and me immediately. While we spent the day with her, Aunt Paula asked us over and over who the tall guy and short woman were who were standing in the corner of her room. Gerry and I didn't see anyone, but my aunt insisted that the couple was there! I've come to believe that they were my dad and mother. Aunt Paula's time was drawing near, and God gave me this to read to her from Psalm 16 NIV:

> "[1]Keep me safe, my God. For in you I take refuge. [2]I say to the LORD, 'you are my LORD; apart from you I have no good thing.' [3]I say of the holy people who are in the land, 'They are the noble ones in whom is all my delight.' [4]Those who run after other gods will suffer more and more. I will not pour out libations of blood to such gods or take up their names on my lips. [5]LORD, you alone are my portion and my cup; you make my lot secure. [6]The boundary lines have fallen for me in pleasant places; surely I have a delightful inheritance. [7]I will praise the LORD, who counsels me; even at night my heart instructs me. [8]I keep my eyes always on the LORD. With him at my right hand, I will not be shaken. [9]Therefore my heart is glad and my tongue rejoices; my body also will rest secure, [10]because you will not abandon me to the realm of the dead, nor will you let your faithful one see decay. [11]You make known to me the path of life; you will fill me with joy in your presence, with eternal pleasures at your right hand."

Through His Word, God was comforting my Aunt Paula, Gerry, and me on what was to come. I assured her it was okay for her to go ahead. God planned for Gerry and me to spend two days to say our final farewells to my lifelong, irreplaceable friend, and I am so thankful for that. God knows that I was not there for my mom and dad the way I should have been, but He gave me another chance to be with my mother's baby sister, my Aunt Paula, who grew up alongside me.

Soon after Aunt Paula's passing, we held a double memorial service in New Jersey for Aunt Paula and her sister Frannie.

Cousins were there that I had not seen for thirty-five years. They remembered me as a spoiled brat who became a wild, alcoholic drug addict, so their heads spun completely around when they saw me as a minister facilitating the memorials. Only by God's grace and power could the changes have occurred in my life! God deserves all the glory, honor, and praise. I am convinced, whole-heartedly, that God's touch on a lost person's life can change the person so radically that it becomes nearly impossible for anyone who knew the person earlier to recognize him or her at all!

My new God-given life of sobriety has blessed me with Gerry, my beautiful, sober wife, and our family totaling a son and daughter, seven grandchildren, and three great grandchildren. God is slowly bringing my son Ari back into my life. At this point in my writing, Ari has told me that he is married now. Identifying as a trans-man, Ari and his wife are expecting a baby girl who will become my granddaughter. I don't know the details of how all of this is happening, so I'm in constant prayer for them believing that God already knows the name of this child, and only He knows what is to come. Jeremiah 1:5 NIV puts it this way, *"Before I formed you in the womb, I knew you;"* God knew my name, as well, before I was born. He watched me walk away from my early teaching about Him, but allowed me to remember my mother's words: *"Run to God and never blame Him when things don't go our way because he's always there."* He let me go my own stubborn, self-centered way, keeping me alive through overdoses, kidney failure, a brain aneurism, seizures, and any other harm that could have been brought on by my destructive self or by the company I was keeping! When I recognized and responded wholeheartedly to His call at the altar on Christmas Eve, 2012, God changed me completely and gave me a new life with great purpose. He did the same with my wife Gerry. I am not bragging about Gerry and me. I'm bragging about what God has done and what He promises to do for those who call to Him and are obedient to His Word. We have become members of the Family of God, a myriad of people who, like Gerry and me, have stories of how God made Himself known to them and drew them to Himself to open their eyes. It's common among us to hear the phrases "Everyone has a story." and "A relationship with Jesus changes everything!" So true.

As required in Celebrate Recovery, I made a list of my own hurts, habits, and hang-ups, which turned out to be very long and, most likely, incomplete: alcohol, drugs, cigarettes, pride, ego, gambling, adultery, lying, stealing, cheating, manipulating, people pleasing, divorce, guilt, anger, codependency, low self-esteem, shame, perfectionism, sarcasm, PTSD, betrayal, fear, verbal abuse, pornography, depression, confusion, attempts at suicide, grief, high anxiety, greed, jealousy, rejection, and impatience—to name a few. Think about it. Families, friendships, individuals, and businesses collapse every day because someone took even one or more of these habits to the extreme! With God, I can deal with these things. I get help daily by working the Twelve Steps of Celebrate Recovery. I remember that if I am not working toward *recovering*, I am working toward *relapsing*, and that a person will repeat what is not repaired!

I see myself as a nobody, but, in essence, I am everybody. Everybody is struggling inside or outside a closet of some kind. Isolation is the devil's playground; that's when and where our stinkin' thinkin' starts. The voice I listen to now is that still, small whisper from God who is with me everywhere. He gathered up my sorrows and failures and gently pulled me aside to let me know that I was headed in the wrong direction. Only faith in Jesus could turn my hopeless end into an endless hope! Through it all, I've learned to trust Him and to love Him more for who He is! I live my days loving to serve Him. I'm latched, like Velcro®, onto His Word, the Bible. He has never failed to keep His promises! My past certainly *was* His training for my future!

> [14]*"Because he loves me, says the LORD, I will rescue him;*
> *I will protect him, for he acknowledges my name.* [15]*He will*
> *call on me, and I will answer him; I will be with him in*
> *trouble, I will deliver him and honor him.* [16]*With long life*
> *I will satisfy him and show him my salvation."*
> Psalm 91: 14–16 NIV

"No eye has seen, no ear has heard, and no mind has imagined what God has prepared for those who love him."
1 Corinthians 2:9 NLT

THE END

www.ingramcontent.com/pod-product-compliance
Lightning Source LLC
Chambersburg PA
CBHW070449090426
42735CB00012B/2491